# BRIGHTON
## RESTAURANT GUIDE
# 2020

# RESTAURANTS, BARS AND CAFES

## Your Guide to Authentic Regional Eats

GUIDE BOOK FOR TOURIST

BRIGHTON RESTAURANT GUIDE 2020
Best Rated Restaurants in Brighton, United Kingdom

ISBN-13: 9781085974554

## BRIGHTON RESTAURANT GUIDE 2020

### Most Recommended Restaurants in Brighton

*This directory is dedicated to Brighton Business Owners and Managers
who provide the experience that the locals and tourists enjoy.
Thanks you very much for all that you do and thank for being the "People Choice".*

*Thanks to everyone that posts their reviews online and
the amazing reviews sites that make our life easier.*

*The places listed in this book are the most positively reviewed
and recommended by locals and travelers from around the world.*

*Thank you for your time and enjoy the directory that is
designed with locals and tourist in mind!*

# TOP 500
# RESTAURANTS
Ranked from #1 to #500

#1
**Iydea**
**Cuisines:** Vegetarian, Cafeteria
**Average price:** Inexpensive
**Address:** 17 Kensington Gardens
Brighton BN1 4AL
**Phone:** +44 1273 667992

#2
**Riddle and Finns**
**Cuisines:** Seafood, Champagne Bar
**Average price:** Expensive
**Address:** 12 Meeting House Lane
Brighton BN1 1HB
**Phone:** +44 1273 721667

#3
**Casa Don Carlos**
**Cuisines:** Spanish, Tapas Bar
**Average price:** Modest
**Address:** 5 Union Street
Brighton BN1 1HA
**Phone:** +44 1273 327177

#4
**The Gingerman**
**Cuisines:** British, Food
**Average price:** Expensive
**Address:** 21a Norfolk Square
Brighton BN1 2PD
**Phone:** +44 1273 326688

#5
**Foodilic**
**Cuisines:** Buffet, Food
**Average price:** Inexpensive
**Address:** 60 North Street
Brighton BN1 1RH
**Phone:** +44 1273 774138

#6
**The Chilli Pickle**
**Cuisines:** Indian
**Average price:** Modest
**Address:** 17 Jubilee Street
Brighton BN1 1GE
**Phone:** +44 1273 900383

#7
**Hop Poles**
**Cuisines:** Pub, British
**Average price:** Modest
**Address:** 13 Middle Street
Brighton BN1 1AL
**Phone:** +44 1273 207566

#8
**Bill's**
**Cuisines:** British, Breakfast & Brunch
**Average price:** Modest
**Address:** 100 North Road
Brighton BN1 1YE
**Phone:** +44 1273 692894

#9
**Basketmakers Arms**
**Cuisines:** Pub, British, Food
**Average price:** Inexpensive
**Address:** 12 Gloucester Road
Brighton BN1 4AD
**Phone:** +44 1273 689006

#10
**La Cave à Fromage**
**Cuisines:** Cheese Shop, French
**Average price:** Modest
**Address:** 34-35 Western Road
Brighton BN3 1AF
**Phone:** +44 1273 725500

#11
**Northern Lights**
**Cuisines:** Scandinavian, Pub
**Average price:** Modest
**Address:** 6 Little E Street
Brighton BN1 1HT
**Phone:** +44 1273 747096

#12
**La Cucina**
**Cuisines:** Pizza, Fast Food, Italian
**Average price:** Modest
**Address:** 4a Montpelier Place
Brighton BN1 3BF
**Phone:** +44 1273 202206

#13
**Pompoko**
**Cuisines:** Japanese
**Average price:** Inexpensive
**Address:** 110 Church Street
Brighton BN1 1UD
**Phone:** +44 7796 001927

#14
**Food For Friends**
**Cuisines:** Vegetarian, Coffee, Tea
**Average price:** Modest
**Address:** 17-18 Prince Albert Street
Brighton BN1 1HF
**Phone:** +44 1273 202310

#15
**Bom-Bane's**
**Cuisines:** Coffee, Tea,
Music Venues, Belgian
**Average price:** Expensive
**Address:** 24 George Street
Brighton BN2 1RH
**Phone:** +44 1273 606400

#16
**Robin Hood**
**Cuisines:** Pub, Pizza
**Average price:** Modest
**Address:** 3 Norfolk Place
Brighton BN1 2PF
**Phone:** +44 1273 325645

#17
**Warung Tujuh**
**Cuisines:** Indonesian, Fast Food
**Average price:** Modest
**Address:** 7 Pool Valley
Brighton BN1 1NJ
**Phone:** +44 1273 720784

#18
**Brighton Burger**
**Cuisines:** Fast Food, British, Burgers
**Average price:** Inexpensive
**Address:** 11a Market Street
Brighton BN1 1HH
**Phone:** +44 1273 205979

#19
**Terre A Terre**
**Cuisines:** Vegetarian, Food
**Average price:** Expensive
**Address:** 71 East Street
Brighton BN1 1HQ
**Phone:** +44 1273 729051

#20
**Sussex Yeoman**
**Cuisines:** Pub, British
**Average price:** Modest
**Address:** 7 Guildford Road
Brighton BN1 3LU
**Phone:** +44 1273 327985

#21
**Sushi Garden**
**Cuisines:** Japanese, Sushi Bar
**Average price:** Expensive
**Address:** 32a-33a Preston Street
Brighton BN1 2HP
**Phone:** +44 1273 727246

#22
**English's of Brighton**
**Cuisines:** Seafood
**Average price:** Expensive
**Address:** 29 East Street
Brighton BN1 1HL
**Phone:** +44 1273 327980

#23
**The Ginger Pig**
**Cuisines:** Gastropub, French
**Average price:** Expensive
**Address:** 3 Hove Street
Brighton BN3 2TR
**Phone:** +44 1273 736123

#24
**Jamie's Italian**
**Cuisines:** Italian
**Average price:** Modest
**Address:** 11 Black Lion St
Brighton BN1 1ND
**Phone:** +44 1273 915480

#25
**Moshimo**
**Cuisines:** Japanese, Sushi Bar
**Average price:** Modest
**Address:** The Opticon Bartholomew Square
Brighton BN1 1JS
**Phone:** +44 1273 719195

#26
**Grubbs Burgers**
**Cuisines:** Fast Food, Burgers, Coffee, Tea
**Average price:** Inexpensive
**Address:** 13 York Place
Brighton BN1 4GU
**Phone:** +44 1273 691869

#27
**Earth And Stars**
**Cuisines:** Gastropub, Pub
**Average price:** Modest
**Address:** 46 Windsor Street
Brighton BN1 1RJ
**Phone:** +44 1273 722879

#28
**Toast**
**Cuisines:** Sandwiches, Coffee, Tea,
Breakfast & Brunch
**Average price:** Inexpensive
**Address:** 38 Trafalgar Street
Brighton BN1 4ED
**Phone:** +44 872 148 6121

#29
**MuraSaki**
**Cuisines:** Japanese, Fast Food
**Average price:** Modest
**Address:** 115 Dyke Road
Brighton BN1 3JE
**Phone:** +44 1273 326231

#30
**Planet India**
**Cuisines:** Indian, Food
**Average price:** Modest
**Address:** 4-5 Richmond Parade
Brighton BN2 9PH
**Phone:** +44 1273 818149

#31
**Cocoa**
**Cuisines:** Desserts, French
**Average price:** Modest
**Address:** 48 Queens Road
Brighton BN1 3XB
**Phone:** +44 1273 777412

#33
**Carlito Burrito**
**Cuisines:** Street Vendor, Mexican
**Average price:** Modest
**Address:** 12 York Place
Brighton BN1 4GU
**Phone:** +44 1273 671191

#32
**Siam Siam**
**Cuisines:** Thai
**Average price:** Modest
**Address:** 73 - 74 Preston Street
Brighton BN1 2HG
**Phone:** +44 1273 757424

#34
**Burger Brothers**
**Cuisines:** Burgers
**Average price:** Inexpensive
**Address:** 97 North Road
Brighton BN1 1YE
**Phone:** +44 1273 706980

#35
**Kensington Cafe**
**Cuisines:** Coffee, Tea,
Breakfast & Brunch, British
**Average price:** Inexpensive
**Address:** 1a Kensington Gardens
Brighton BN1 4AL
**Phone:** +44 1273 570963

#36
**E-Kagen Sushi & Noodle Bar**
**Cuisines:** Japanese
**Average price:** Inexpensive
**Address:** 22-23 Sydney Street
Brighton BN1 4EN
**Phone:** +44 1273 687068

#37
**The Windmill**
**Cuisines:** Pub, British
**Average price:** Modest
**Address:** 69 Upper North Street
Brighton BN1 3FL
**Phone:** +44 1273 202475

#38
**Mange Tout**
**Cuisines:** French, Breakfast & Brunch
**Average price:** Modest
**Address:** 81 Trafalgar Street
Brighton BN1 4EB
**Phone:** +44 1273 607270

#39
**Sawadee**
**Cuisines:** Thai
**Average price:** Modest
**Address:** 87 ST. James's Street
Brighton BN2 1TP
**Phone:** +44 1273 624233

#40
**Regency Restaurant**
**Cuisines:** Seafood
**Average price:** Modest
**Address:** 131 Kings Road
Brighton BN1 2HH
**Phone:** +44 1273 325014

#41
**The Setting Sun**
**Cuisines:** Pub, Gastropub
**Average price:** Modest
**Address:** 1 Windmill Street
Brighton BN2 0GN
**Phone:** +44 1273 626192

#42
**Sam's Of
Brighton**
**Cuisines:** British, Breakfast & Brunch
**Average price:** Modest
**Address:** 1 Paston Place
Brighton BN2 1HA
**Phone:** +44 1273 676222

#43
**Muang Thai Restaurant**
**Cuisines:** Thai, Food
**Average price:** Modest
**Address:** 77 St James's Street
Brighton BN2 1PA
**Phone:** +44 1273 605223

#44
**Bona Foodie**
**Cuisines:** Deli, Coffee, Tea, Sandwiches
**Average price:** Exclusive
**Address:** 21 ST James's Street
Brighton BN2 1RF
**Phone:** +44 1273 698007

#45
**Grubbs Burgers**
**Cuisines:** Fast Food, Burgers, Coffee, Tea
**Average price:** Modest
**Address:** 89 St James's Street
Brighton BN2 1TP
**Phone:** +44 1273 688111

#46
**Browns Bar & Brasserie**
**Cuisines:** British
**Average price:** Expensive
**Address:** 3-4 Duke Street
Brighton BN1 1AH
**Phone:** +44 1273 323501

#47
**Agra Tandoori Take Away**
**Cuisines:** Fast Food, Indian
**Average price:** Modest
**Address:** 263 Ditchling Road
Brighton BN1 6JH
**Phone:** +44 1273 541652

#48
**Bardsley's Fish & Chips**
**Cuisines:** Fish & Chips
**Average price:** Modest
**Address:** 22-23a Baker Street
Brighton BN1 4JN
**Phone:** +44 1273 681256

#49
**River Spice**
**Cuisines:** Indian
**Average price:** Modest
**Address:** 17 Preston Street
Brighton BN1 2HN
**Phone:** +44 1273 739183

#50
**Alfresco**
**Cuisines:** Italian, Coffee, Tea
**Average price:** Expensive
**Address:** Kings Road Arches
Brighton BN1 2LN
**Phone:** +44 1273 206523

#51
**Pizzaface**
**Cuisines:** Pizza, Fast Food
**Average price:** Modest
**Address:** 35 St Georges Road
Brighton BN2 1ED
**Phone:** +44 1273 699082

#52
**The Prince George**
**Cuisines:** British, Pub, Vegetarian
**Average price:** Modest
**Address:** 5 Trafalgar Street
Brighton BN1 4EQ
**Phone:** +44 1273 681055

#53
**The Foragers**
**Cuisines:** Gastropub, Pub, British
**Average price:** Modest
**Address:** 3 Stirling Place
Brighton BN3 3YU
**Phone:** +44 1273 733134

#54
**The Dorset**
**Cuisines:** Seafood, Pub
**Average price:** Modest
**Address:** 28 North Road
Brighton BN1 1YB
**Phone:** +44 1273 605423

#55
**Krua Anne**
**Cuisines:** Thai
**Average price:** Inexpensive
**Address:** 19 Kensington Gardens
Brighton BN1 4AL
**Phone:** +44 1273 628555

#56
**Mascara Restaurant**
**Cuisines:** African
**Average price:** Modest
**Address:** 101 Western Road
Brighton BN1 2AA
**Phone:** +44 1273 278185

#57
**Billie's**
**Cuisines:** Breakfast & Brunch
**Average price:** Inexpensive
**Address:** 34 Hampton Place
Brighton BN1 3DD
**Phone:** +44 1273 774386

#58
**Saint James**
**Cuisines:** Pub, Thai
**Average price:** Modest
**Address:** 16 Madeira Place
Brighton BN2 1TN
**Phone:** +44 1273 626696

#59
**Fortune of War**
**Cuisines:** Pub, Lounge, British
**Average price:** Modest
**Address:** 157 Kings Road Arches
Brighton BN1 1NB
**Phone:** +44 1273 205065

#60
**Estia**
**Cuisines:** Greek, Mediterranean, Caterer
**Average price:** Modest
**Address:** 3 Hampton Place
Brighton BN1 3DA
**Phone:** +44 1273 777399

#61
**The Medicine Chest**
**Cuisines:** American, European
**Average price:** Expensive
**Address:** 51 - 55 Brunswick Street
Brighton BN3 1AU
**Phone:** +44 1273 770002

#62
**Melrose**
**Cuisines:** Seafood
**Average price:** Modest
**Address:** 132 Kings Road
Brighton BN1 2HH
**Phone:** +44 1273 326520

#63
**Caffe Aldo**
**Cuisines:** Italian, Pizza, Fast Food
**Average price:** Inexpensive
**Address:** 77 Trafalgar Street
Brighton BN1 4EB
**Phone:** +44 1273 819181

#64
**Fishy Fishy**
**Cuisines:** Seafood
**Average price:** Expensive
**Address:** 36 East St
Brighton BN1 1HL
**Phone:** +44 1273 723750

#65
**The Coal Shed**
**Cuisines:** Barbeque
**Average price:** Expensive
**Address:** 8 Boyces Street
Brighton BN1 1AN
**Phone:** +44 1273 322998

#66
**Temptation**
**Cuisines:** Breakfast & Brunch,
Coffee, Tea, Café
**Average price:** Modest
**Address:** 56 Gardner Street
Brighton BN1 1UN
**Phone:** +44 1273 673045

#67
**Pavel**
**Cuisines:** Indian
**Average price:** Modest
**Address:** 40 St James Street
Brighton BN2 1RG
**Phone:** +44 1273 692711

#68
**The Greys**
**Cuisines:** Pub, British
**Average price:** Modest
**Address:** 105 Southover Street
Brighton BN2 9UA
**Phone:** +44 1273 680734

#69
**Black Lion**
**Cuisines:** Pub, Gastropub, British
**Average price:** Modest
**Address:** 14 Black Lion Street
Brighton BN1 1ND
**Phone:** +44 1273 711884

#70
**The Old Bank**
**Cuisines:** Steakhouse
**Average price:** Expensive
**Address:** 120 St George's Road
Brighton BN2 1EA
**Phone:** +44 1273 682200

#71
**The Chimney House**
**Cuisines:** Gastropub, Pub, British
**Average price:** Expensive
**Address:** 28 Upper Hamilton Road
Brighton BN1 5DF
**Phone:** +44 1273 556708

#72
**Plateau**
**Cuisines:** Wine Bar, French, Tapas
**Average price:** Expensive
**Address:** 1 Bartholomews
Brighton BN1 1HG
**Phone:** +44 1273 733085

#73
**Rock Ola**
**Cuisines:** American, Café
**Average price:** Modest
**Address:** 29 Tidy Street
Brighton BN1 4EL
**Phone:** +44 1273 673744

#74
**The Restaurant At Drakes**
**Cuisines:** European
**Average price:** Exclusive
**Address:** 43-44 Marine Parade
Brighton BN2 1PE
**Phone:** +44 1273 696934

#75
**Blenio Bistro**
**Cuisines:** French, Coffee, Tea
**Average price:** Modest
**Address:** 87 - 93 Dyke Road
Brighton BN1 3JE
**Phone:** +44 1273 220220

#76
**The Daily Catch**
**Cuisines:** Fast Food, Seafood
**Average price:** Modest
**Address:** 102 St James's Street
Brighton BN2 1TP
**Phone:** +44 1273 571233

#77
**Olé Olé**
**Cuisines:** Tapas Bar, Steakhouse,
Spanish, Tapas
**Average price:** Modest
**Address:** 42 Meeting House Lane
Brighton BN1 1HB
**Phone:** +44 1273 739939

#78
**Red Snapper**
**Cuisines:** Thai
**Average price:** Modest
**Address:** 90 Dyke Road
Brighton BN1 3JD
**Phone:** +44 1273 778866

#79
**Harry Ramsden's**
**Cuisines:** Fish & Chips
**Average price:** Inexpensive
**Address:** 1-4 Marine Parade
Brighton BN2 1PA
**Phone:** +44 1273 690691

#80
**Open House**
**Cuisines:** Pub, Gastropub
**Average price:** Modest
**Address:** 146 Springfield Road
Brighton BN1 6BZ
**Phone:** +44 1273 880102

#81
**Las Iguanas**
**Cuisines:** Lounge, Mexican, Brazilian
**Average price:** Modest
**Address:** 7-8 Jubilee Street
Brighton BN1 1GE
**Phone:** +44 1273 573550

#82
**Buddies Restaurant**
**Cuisines:** Fish & Chips, Fast Food, Café
**Average price:** Modest
**Address:** 46 Kings Rd
Brighton BN1 1NA
**Phone:** +44 1273 323600

#83
**Mai Ped Ped Ped**
**Cuisines:** Thai, Tapas
**Average price:** Expensive
**Address:** 11a Market Street
Brighton BN1 1HH
**Phone:** +44 1273 737373

#84
**Coach House**
**Cuisines:** British
**Average price:** Modest
**Address:** 59 Middle Street
Brighton BN1 1AL
**Phone:** +44 1273 719000

#85
**Bombay Aloo**
**Cuisines:** Vegetarian, Indian
**Average price:** Inexpensive
**Address:** 39 Ship Street
Brighton BN1 1AB
**Phone:** +44 1273 771089

#86
**Fountain Head**
**Cuisines:** Pub, Gastropub
**Average price:** Modest
**Address:** 101-103 North Road
Brighton BN1 1YE
**Phone:** +44 1273 628091

#87
**Little Bay Restaurant**
**Cuisines:** European, French, Mediterranean
**Average price:** Modest
**Address:** 60-64 Kings Road
Brighton BN1 1NA
**Phone:** +44 1273 731330

#88
**The New Club**
**Cuisines:** Food, Cocktail Bar, American
**Average price:** Modest
**Address:** 133-134 Kings Road
Brighton BN1 2HH
**Phone:** +44 1273 730320

#89
**Pho**
**Cuisines:** Vietnamese
**Average price:** Modest
**Address:** 12 Black Lion Street
Brighton BN1 1ND
**Phone:** +44 1273 202403

#90
**Solera**
**Cuisines:** Spanish, Wine Bar, Tapas
**Average price:** Modest
**Address:** 42 Sydney Street
Brighton BN1 4EP
**Phone:** +44 1273 673966

#91
**Blackbird Tea Rooms**
**Cuisines:** Tea Room, Coffee, Tea, Café
**Average price:** Modest
**Address:** 30 Ship Street
Brighton BN1 1AD
**Phone:** +44 1273 249454

#92
**L'Église**
**Cuisines:** French
**Average price:** Expensive
**Address:** 196 Church Road
Brighton BN3 2DJ
**Phone:** +44 1273 220868

#93
**New Steine Bistro**
**Cuisines:** French, Breakfast & Brunch, British
**Average price:** Modest
**Address:** 10 - 11 New Steine
Brighton BN2 1PB
**Phone:** +44 1273 695415

#94
**JB's American Diner**
**Cuisines:** American
**Average price:** Modest
**Address:** 31 Kings Road
Brighton BN1 1NR
**Phone:** +44 1273 771776

#95
**Istanbul Restaurant**
**Cuisines:** Specialty Food, Fast Food, Turkish
**Average price:** Inexpensive
**Address:** 125 Western Rd
Brighton BN1 2AD
**Phone:** +44 1273 326699

#96
**Uncle Sams Hamburger Express**
**Cuisines:** Fast Food, Burgers
**Average price:** Inexpensive
**Address:** 4A Montpelier Road
Brighton BN1 2LQ
**Phone:** +44 1273 324065

#97
**The House**
**Cuisines:** British, Mediterranean
**Average price:** Expensive
**Address:** 37 East Street
Brighton BN1 1HL
**Phone:** +44 1273 321111

#98
**Pub With No Name**
**Cuisines:** Pub, Gastropub
**Average price:** Modest
**Address:** 58 Southover Street
Brighton BN2 9UF
**Phone:** +44 1273 601419

#99
**Moksha Caffe**
**Cuisines:** Coffee, Tea, Sandwiches, Bakery
**Average price:** Inexpensive
**Address:** 4-5 York Placce
Brighton BN1 4GU
**Phone:** +44 1273 248890

#100
**Market Diner**
**Cuisines:** Diner, Fast Food
**Average price:** Inexpensive
**Address:** 19-21 Circus Street
Brighton BN2 9QF
**Phone:** +44 1273 608273

#101
**Good Companions**
**Cuisines:** Pub, Gastropub
**Average price:** Inexpensive
**Address:** 132 Dyke Road
Brighton BN1 3TE
**Phone:** +44 1273 202062

#102
**Ginger Dog**
**Cuisines:** British
**Average price:** Modest
**Address:** 12 College Pl
Brighton BN2 1HN
**Phone:** +44 1273 620990

#103
**The Cod Father**
**Cuisines:** Fish & Chips
**Average price:** Inexpensive
**Address:** 109 Islingword Road
Brighton BN2 9SG
**Phone:** +44 1273 699038

#104
**MEATliquor**
**Brighton**
**Cuisines:** American, Burgers, Cheesesteaks
**Average price:** Modest
**Address:** 22-23 York Place
Brighton BN1 4GU
**Phone:** +44 1273 917710

#105
**Shahi Tandoori**
**Cuisines:** Indian, Pakistani
**Average price:** Modest
**Address:** 40-42 Beaconsfield Road
Brighton BN1 4QH
**Phone:** +44 1273 626187

#106
**Archipelagos**
**Cuisines:** Greek
**Average price:** Modest
**Address:** 121 Western Road
Brighton BN3 1DB
**Phone:** +44 1273 779474

#107
**Wild Cherry**
**Cuisines:** Deli, Coffee, Tea
**Average price:** Modest
**Address:** 91 Queens Park Road
Brighton BN2 0GJ
**Phone:** +44 1273 691494

#108
**Druid's Head**
**Cuisines:** Pub, Gastropub
**Average price:** Modest
**Address:** 9 Brighton Place
Brighton BN1 1HJ
**Phone:** +44 1273 325490

#109
**Harvester**
**Cuisines:** Steakhouse
**Average price:** Modest
**Address:** 1 Madeira Drive
Brighton BN2 1PS
**Phone:** +44 1273 573730

#110
**Circus Circus**
**Cuisines:** Pub, Thai
**Average price:** Modest
**Address:** 2 Preston Road
Brighton BN1 4QF
**Phone:** +44 1273 620026

#111
**Madame Geisha**
**Cuisines:** Asian Fusion, Dance Club
**Average price:** Modest
**Address:** 75 - 79 East St
Brighton BN1 1NF
**Phone:** +44 1273 770847

#112
**Si Signore**
**Cuisines:** Italian
**Average price:** Modest
**Address:** 12 Sydney Street
Brighton BN1 4EN
**Phone:** +44 1273 671266

#113
**Bath Arms**
**Cuisines:** Pub, British, Coffee, Tea
**Average price:** Modest
**Address:** 4 Meeting House Lane
Brighton BN1 1HB
**Phone:** +44 1273 731864

#114
**The Gladstone**
**Cuisines:** Pub, British, Music Venues
**Average price:** Inexpensive
**Address:** 123 Lewes Road
Brighton BN2 3QB
**Phone:** +44 4412 7362 0888

#115
**Wagamama**
**Cuisines:** Japanese
**Average price:** Expensive
**Address:** 93 North Road
Brighton BN1 1YE
**Phone:** +44 1273 688892

#116
**The Laine Deli**
**Cuisines:** Coffee, Tea, Café, Sandwiches
**Average price:** Inexpensive
**Address:** 31 Trafalgar Street
Brighton BN1 4ED
**Phone:** +44 1273 686665

#117
**The Signalman**
**Cuisines:** Pub, Gastropub
**Average price:** Modest
**Address:** 76 Ditchling Rise
Brighton BN1 4QQ
**Phone:** +44 1273 689783

#118
**Steki's Taverna**
**Cuisines:** Greek, Mediterranean, Fast Food
**Average price:** Expensive
**Address:** 127 Kings Road
Brighton BN1 2FA
**Phone:** +44 1273 730202

#119
**El Mexicano**
**Cuisines:** Mexican, Tex-Mex
**Average price:** Modest
**Address:** 7 New Road
Brighton BN1 1UF
**Phone:** +44 1273 727766

#120
**Cote**
**Cuisines:** Restaurant
**Average price:** Expensive
**Address:** 115-116 Church Street
Brighton BN1 1UP
**Phone:** +44 1273 687541

#121
**Pavilion Gardens Cafe**
**Cuisines:** Coffee, Tea, Sandwiches, Desserts
**Average price:** Inexpensive
**Address:** New Road
Brighton BN1 1UG
**Phone:** +44 1273 730712

#122
**Pinocchio**
**Cuisines:** Italian, Pizza
**Average price:** Inexpensive
**Address:** 22 New Road
Brighton BN1 1UF
**Phone:** +44 1273 677676

#123
**Al Rouche**
**Cuisines:** Lebanese
**Average price:** Inexpensive
**Address:** 44 Preston St
Brighton BN1 2HP
**Phone:** +44 1273 734810

#124
**Mad Hatter Cafe**
**Cuisines:** Coffee, Tea,
Breakfast & Brunch, Juice Bar
**Average price:** Inexpensive
**Address:** 35 Montpelier Rd
Brighton BN1 3BA
**Phone:** +44 1273 722279

#125
**Los Taquitos**
**Cuisines:** Mexican, Fast Food
**Average price:** Inexpensive
**Address:** 6 York Place
Brighton BN1 4GU
**Phone:** +44 1273 628630

#126
**The Galley**
**Cuisines:** Crêperie, Sandwiches
**Average price:** Inexpensive
**Address:** 9 Church Street
Brighton BN1 1US
**Phone:** +44 1273 724499

#127
**Zizzi**
**Cuisines:** Italian, Pizza
**Average price:** Modest
**Address:** 7-8 Prince Albert Street
Brighton BN1 1HE
**Phone:** +44 1273 323273

#128
**Farm**
**Cuisines:** Coffee, Tea, Desserts,
Breakfast & Brunch
**Average price:** Modest
**Address:** 99 North Road
Brighton BN1 1YE
**Phone:** +44 1273 623143

#129
**Chilka House**
**Cuisines:** Chinese
**Average price:** Modest
**Address:** 15 Baker Street
Brighton BN1 4JN
**Phone:** +44 1273 677085

#130
**Fiddler's Elbow**
**Cuisines:** Irish, Pub
**Average price:** Modest
**Address:** 11 Boyces Street
Brighton BN1 1AN
**Phone:** +44 1273 325850

#131
**Grints of Brighton**
**Cuisines:** Coffee, Tea, Bakery, Café
**Average price:** Inexpensive
**Address:** 13 Cranbourne Street
Brighton BN1 2RD
**Phone:** +44 1273 728091

#132
**TFI Lunch**
**Cuisines:** Breakfast & Brunch,
Sandwiches, Coffee, Tea
**Average price:** Inexpensive
**Address:** 56 Queens Road
Brighton BN1 3XD
**Phone:** +44 1273 208292

#133
**FilFil Cafe**
**Cuisines:** Middle Eastern, Fast Food
**Average price:** Inexpensive
**Address:** 21 Gardner Street
Brighton BN1 1UP
**Phone:** +44 1273 696289

#134
**Koba**
**Cuisines:** Cocktail Bar,
Breakfast & Brunch, Café
**Average price:** Expensive
**Address:** 135 Western Road
Brighton BN1 2LA
**Phone:** +44 1273 720059

#135
**Giggling Squid**
**Cuisines:** Thai
**Average price:** Modest
**Address:** 11 Market St
Brighton BN1 1HH
**Phone:** +44 1273 737373

#136
**Good Friends**
**Cuisines:** Chinese
**Average price:** Modest
**Address:** 24-25 Preston Street
Brighton BN1 2HN
**Phone:** +44 1273 779836

#137
**Cafe Rouge**
**Cuisines:** Coffee, Tea, French
**Average price:** Modest
**Address:** 24 Prince Albert St
Brighton BN1 1HF
**Phone:** +44 1273 774422

#138
**The Arrogant Frog Brasserie**
**Cuisines:** French
**Average price:** Exclusive
**Address:** 64 Kings Road
Brighton BN1 1NA
**Phone:** +44 1273 721488

#139
**Twisted Lemon**
**Cuisines:** Restaurant, Cocktail Bar
**Average price:** Inexpensive
**Address:** 41 Middle Street
Brighton BN1 1AL
**Phone:** +44 1273 726693

#140
**Cafe Coho**
**Cuisines:** Breakfast & Brunch,
Café, Coffee, Tea
**Average price:** Modest
**Address:** 53 Ship Street
Brighton BN1 1AF
**Phone:** +44 1273 747777

#141
**Bankers Restaurant**
**Cuisines:** Fish & Chips, Seafood
**Average price:** Modest
**Address:** 116a Western Road
Brighton BN1 2AB
**Phone:** +44 1273 328267

#142
**Seven Stars**
**Cuisines:** Pub, Gastropub
**Average price:** Modest
**Address:** 27 Ship St
Brighton BN1 1AD
**Phone:** +44 1273 258800

#143
**Coast to Coast**
**Cuisines:** American, American
**Average price:** Expensive
**Address:** 3 Waterfront
Brighton BN2 5WA
**Phone:** +44 1273 626170

#144
**The Station Pub**
**Cuisines:** Bar, Pizza
**Average price:** Modest
**Address:** 100 Goldstone Villas
Brighton BN3 3RU
**Phone:** +44 1273 733660

#145
**Casalingo**
**Cuisines:** Italian, Seafood
**Average price:** Inexpensive
**Address:** 29 Preston Street
Brighton BN1 2HP
**Phone:** +44 1273 328775

#146
**Okinami**
**Cuisines:** Japanese, Sushi Bar
**Average price:** Expensive
**Address:** 6 New Road
Brighton BN1 1UF
**Phone:** +44 1273 773777

#147
**Murasaki Bento**
**Cuisines:** Sushi Bar
**Average price:** Modest
**Address:** 16 Montpelier Place
Brighton BN1 3BF
**Phone:** +44 1273 775771

#148
**Thai Pad Thai**
**Cuisines:** Thai
**Average price:** Inexpensive
**Address:** 72 Dyke Road
Brighton BN1 7JD
**Phone:** +44 1273 737878

#149
**Nishat Tandoori**
**Cuisines:** Indian, Fast Food
**Average price:** Modest
**Address:** 58 Preston St
Brighton BN1 2
**Phone:** +44 1273 321701

#150
**Bhindis**
**Cuisines:** Indian, Fast Food
**Average price:** Modest
**Address:** 166 Lewes Road
Brighton BN2 3LD
**Phone:** +44 1273 690390

#151
**Park View**
**Cuisines:** Pub, British
**Average price:** Modest
**Address:** 71 Preston Drove
Brighton BN1 6LD
**Phone:** +44 1273 541663

#152
**Sri India**
**Cuisines:** Indian, Pakistani
**Average price:** Modest
**Address:** 1-2 Wilmington Parade
Brighton BN1 8JJ
**Phone:** +44 1273 330222

#153
**Bodega D Tapa**
**Cuisines:** Tapas Bar
**Average price:** Modest
**Address:** 111 Church St
Brighton BN1 1
**Phone:** +44 1273 674116

#154
**Buddys**
**Cuisines:** Fish & Chips
**Average price:** Modest
**Address:** 50 Kings Road
Brighton BN1 1NA
**Phone:** +44 1273 220313

#155
**Al Nakhl**
**Cuisines:** Turkish
**Average price:** Exclusive
**Address:** 48 West Street
Brighton BN1 2RA
**Phone:** +44 1273 732832

#156
**Pizza Express Restaurants**
**Cuisines:** Pizza, Italian
**Average price:** Modest
**Address:** 4 Waterfront
Brighton BN2 5WA
**Phone:** +44 1273 689300

#157
**Pizza & Pasta Brasserie**
**Cuisines:** Italian
**Average price:** Modest
**Address:** 49 St James's Street
Brighton BN2 1RG
**Phone:** +44 1273 604060

#158
**Fanny's of Hanover**
**Cuisines:** Bakery, Coffee, Tea, Deli
**Average price:** Expensive
**Address:** 135 Islingword Road
Brighton BN2 9SH
**Phone:** +44 1273 670779

#159
**Buffet Island**
**Cuisines:** Chinese, Buffet
**Average price:** Modest
**Address:** 18 York Place
Brighton BN1 4GU
**Phone:** +44 1273 698606

#160
**Aberdeen Steak House**
**Cuisines:** British
**Average price:** Modest
**Address:** 27-28 Preston Street
Brighton BN1 2HP
**Phone:** +44 1273 326892

#161

**Brighton Bystander**
**Cuisines:** Coffee, Tea, Breakfast & Brunch
**Average price:** Expensive
**Address:** 1 Terminus Road
Brighton BN1 3PD
**Phone:** +44 1273 329364

#162
**Gourmet Burger Kitchen**
**Cuisines:** American, Burgers
**Average price:** Modest
**Address:** 44-47 Gardner Street
Brighton BN1 1UN
**Phone:** +44 1273 685895

#163
**Lovefit Cafe**
**Cuisines:** Juice Bar, Coffee, Tea,
Breakfast & Brunch
**Average price:** Expensive
**Address:** 14
Brighton Sq
Brighton BN1 1HD
**Phone:** +44 1273 777941

#164
**Ground Coffee House**
**Cuisines:** Coffee, Tea, Breakfast & Brunch
**Average price:** Modest
**Address:** 36 St Georges Road
Brighton BN2 1ED
**Phone:** +44 1273 696441

#165
**Aguadulce**
**Cuisines:** Spanish, Tapas Bar
**Average price:** Modest
**Address:** 10-11 King's Road
Brighton BN1 1NE
**Phone:** +44 1273 328672

#166
**Chopstick Express**
**Cuisines:** Fast Food
**Average price:** Exclusive
**Address:** 28 Baker Street
Brighton BN1 4JN
**Phone:** +44 1273 609408

#167
**China Garden**
**Cuisines:** Chinese
**Average price:** Expensive
**Address:** 24 Preston Road
Brighton BN1 4QF
**Phone:** +44 1273 696900

#168
**Sofias**
**Cuisines:** Italian
**Average price:** Inexpensive
**Address:** 24 Ship St
Brighton BN1 1AD
**Phone:** +44 1273 321233

#169
**Ottoman Shisha Bar**
**Cuisines:** Turkish, Hookah Bar
**Average price:** Modest
**Address:** 35-38 Lewes Road
Brighton BN2 3HQ
**Phone:** +44 1273 605314

#170
**Pizza Express**
**Cuisines:** Italian, Pizza
**Average price:** Modest
**Address:** Jubilee Street
Brighton BN1 1GE
**Phone:** +44 1273 697691

#171
**Aysha Tandoori**
**Cuisines:** Indian, Pakistani
**Average price:** Inexpensive
**Address:** 7 Oxford St
Brighton BN1 4LA
**Phone:** +44 1273 608885

#172
**Itsu**
**Cuisines:** Asian Fusion, Sushi Bar
**Average price:** Inexpensive
**Address:** 68-70 N Street
Brighton BN1 2RE
**Phone:** +44 1273 830900

#173
**Kambi's Restaurant**
**Cuisines:** Middle Eastern
**Average price:** Modest
**Address:** 107 Western Road
Brighton BN1 2AA
**Phone:** +44 1273 327934

#174
**Thai Spice Restaurant**
**Cuisines:** Thai
**Average price:** Inexpensive
**Address:** 13 Boyces Street
Brighton BN1 1AN
**Phone:** +44 1273 325195

#175
**The Constant Service**
**Cuisines:** Pub, British
**Average price:** Modest
**Address:** 96 Islingword Rd
Brighton BN2 9
**Phone:** +44 1273 607058

#176
**Costa Coffee**
**Cuisines:** Coffee, Tea, Sandwiches
**Average price:** Modest
**Address:** 32 Bond Street
Brighton BN1 1
**Phone:** +44 1273 772024

#177
**Kitchen Cafe**
**Cuisines:** Coffee, Tea,
Breakfast & Brunch, British
**Average price:** Inexpensive
**Address:** 93 Trafalgar Street
Brighton BN1 4ER
**Phone:** +44 1273 674672

#178
**Wagamama**
**Cuisines:** Japanese
**Average price:** Modest
**Address:** 30 Kensington Street
Brighton BN41 2HD
**Phone:** +44 1273 688892

#179
**The Hartington**
**Cuisines:** Pub, Gastropub
**Average price:** Modest
**Address:** 41 Whippingham Road
Brighton BN2 3PF
**Phone:** +44 1273 682874

#180
**Lucky Beach**
**Cuisines:** Burgers
**Average price:** Inexpensive
**Address:** 183 Kings Road Arches
Brighton BN1 1NB
**Phone:** +44 7447 464222

#181
**The Brasserie**
**Cuisines:** Italian, Bar
**Average price:** Modest
**Address:** 15d The Village Square Shops
Brighton BN2 5WA
**Phone:** +44 1273 818026

#182
**The Manor**
**Cuisines:** Breakfast & Brunch, Sandwiches
**Average price:** Modest
**Address:** 52 Gardner St
Brighton BN1 1UN
**Phone:** +44 1273 691700

#183
**Pizza Me A Slice For You**
**Cuisines:** Pizza
**Average price:** Inexpensive
**Address:** The Kiosk Elm Grove
Brighton BN2
**Phone:** +44 1273 622210

#184
**Seven Dials**
**Cuisines:** British
**Average price:** Expensive
**Address:** 1 Buckingham Place
Brighton BN3 1UH
**Phone:** +44 1273 701222

#185
**Lucky Star**
**Cuisines:** Chinese, Buffet
**Average price:** Inexpensive
**Address:** 101 Trafalgar Street
Brighton BN1 4ER
**Phone:** +44 1273 687064

#186
**Caffe Nero**
**Cuisines:** Coffee, Tea, Sandwiches
**Average price:** Modest
**Address:** 39-40 Bond St
Brighton BN1 1RD
**Phone:** +44 1273 723912

#187
**Bagelman**
**Cuisines:** Sandwiches, Bagels, Coffee, Tea
**Average price:** Expensive
**Address:** 31 Ship St
Brighton BN1 1AD
**Phone:** +44 1273 772779

#188
**Carluccio's**
**Cuisines:** Italian, Coffee, Tea
**Average price:** Modest
**Address:** Jubilee Street
Brighton BN1 1GE
**Phone:** +44 1273 690493

#189
**AA Charcoal Grill**
**Cuisines:** Turkish, Barbeque
**Average price:** Inexpensive
**Address:** 41 Lewes Rd
Brighton BN2 3HQ
**Phone:** +44 1273 571003

#190
**Misty's**
**Cuisines:** British, Lounge
**Average price:** Modest
**Address:** 116 Church Rd
Brighton BN3 2EA
**Phone:** +44 1273 220302

#191
**Ohso Social**
**Cuisines:** British, Coffee, Tea, Bar
**Average price:** Modest
**Address:** 250a Kings Rd Arches
Brighton BN1 1NB
**Phone:** +44 1273 746067

#192
**Jade**
**Cuisines:** Chinese, Japanese, Fast Food
**Average price:** Modest
**Address:** 29 Western Rd
Brighton BN3 1AF
**Phone:** +44 1273 778180

#193
**Mo:Mo Dumpling Bar**
**Cuisines:** Tea Room
**Average price:** Modest
**Address:** 15A Kensington Gardens
Brighton BN1 4AL
**Phone:** +44 1273 698129

#194
**Forfars Fresh**
**Cuisines:** Bakery, Sandwiches
**Average price:** Inexpensive
**Address:** 12a Imperial Arcade
Brighton BN1 3EA
**Phone:** +44 1273 325807

#195
**Kokoro**
**Cuisines:** Sushi Bar
**Average price:** Inexpensive
**Address:** 57 North Street
Brighton BN1 1RH
**Phone:** +44 1273 771292

#196
**Darcy's Restaurant**
**Cuisines:** Seafood, British
**Average price:** Expensive
**Address:** 49 Market Street
Brighton BN1 1HH
**Phone:** +44 1273 325560

#197
**Toasters**
**Cuisines:** Do-It-Yourself Food, Fast Food
**Average price:** Modest
**Address:** 12 Market Street
Brighton BN1 1HH
**Phone:** +44 7976 656293

#198
**Nordic Coffee Collective**
**Cuisines:** Café
**Average price:** Inexpensive
**Address:** 16 York Place
Brighton BN1 4GU
**Phone:** +44 1273 673070

#199
**La Marinade**
**Cuisines:** French, European
**Average price:** Expensive
**Address:** 77 St Georges Road
Brighton BN2 1EF
**Phone:** +44 1273 600992

#200
**Bella Napoli**
**Cuisines:** Italian
**Average price:** Modest
**Address:** 19 Waterfront
Brighton BN2 5WA
**Phone:** +44 1273 818577

#201
**Mumbai Express**
**Cuisines:** Indian
**Average price:** Modest
**Address:** 17 sutherland rd
Brighton BN2 0EQ
**Phone:** +44 1273 676005

#202
**Strada**
**Cuisines:** Italian, Pizza
**Average price:** Modest
**Address:** 160-161 North Street
Brighton BN1 1EZ
**Phone:** +44 1273 202070

#203
**The Pond**
**Cuisines:** Thai, Pub
**Average price:** Modest
**Address:** 49 Gloucester Road
Brighton BN1 4AQ
**Phone:** +44 1273 621400

#204
**La Choza**
**Cuisines:** Mexican
**Average price:** Inexpensive
**Address:** 36 Gloucester Road
Brighton BN1 4AP
**Phone:** +44 1273 945926

#205
**Eastern Eye**
**Cuisines:** Indian, Ethnic Food
**Average price:** Modest
**Address:** 58 London Road
Brighton BN1 4JE
**Phone:** +44 1273 685151

#206
**The Buccaneer**
**Cuisines:** Coffee, Tea, Breakfast & Brunch
**Average price:** Inexpensive
**Address:** 186 Kings Road Arches
Brighton BN1 1NB
**Phone:** +44 1273 321393

#207
**New Lotus**
**Cuisines:** Fast Food, Chinese
**Average price:** Expensive
**Address:** 107 Dyke Road
Brighton BN1 3JE
**Phone:** +44 1273 326336

#208
**Magic Wok**
**Cuisines:** Fast Food, Chinese
**Average price:** Modest
**Address:** 49 Preston St
Brighton BN1 2HP
**Phone:** +44 1273 327788

#209
**Oriental Takeaway**
**Cuisines:** Fast Food, Chinese
**Average price:** Modest
**Address:** 70 Lewes Road
Brighton BN2 3HZ
**Phone:** +44 1273 683543

#210
**GNC**
**Cuisines:** Deli
**Average price:** Expensive
**Address:** Churchill Square
Brighton BN1 2TD
**Phone:** +44 1273 710150

#211
**Shakespeares Head**
**Cuisines:** Pub, British
**Average price:** Modest
**Address:** 1 Chatham Place
Brighton BN1 3TP
**Phone:** +44 1273 329444

#212
**The Stoneham**
**Cuisines:** Pub, Pizza
**Average price:** Exclusive
**Address:** 153 Portland Road
Brighton BN3
**Phone:** +44 1273 383840

#213
**Beach House Cafe**
**Cuisines:** Sandwiches, Coffee,
Tea, Ice Cream
**Average price:** Inexpensive
**Address:** 21 King's Road Arches
Brighton BN1 2LN
**Phone:** +44 872 148 6446

#214
**Nandos Chickenland**
**Cuisines:** Portuguese
**Average price:** Modest
**Address:** 34 Duke Street
Brighton BN1 1AG
**Phone:** +44 1273 725483

#215
**Bella Italia Restaurants**
**Cuisines:** Italian
**Average price:** Modest
**Address:** 24 Market Street
Brighton BN1 1HH
**Phone:** +44 1273 777607

#216
**Ganges**
**Cuisines:** Indian, Lounge
**Average price:** Modest
**Address:** 93 Church Rd
Brighton BN3 2BA
**Phone:** +44 1273 728292

#217
**McDonald's**
**Cuisines:** Fast Food
**Average price:** Exclusive
**Address:**
Brighton Marina Village
Brighton BN2 5UT
**Phone:** +44 1273 819111

#218
**Subway**
**Cuisines:** Sandwiches
**Average price:** Inexpensive
**Address:** 146 North Street
Brighton BN1 1RE
**Phone:** +44 1273 236059

#219
**Seagull Restaurant**
**Cuisines:** Seafood
**Average price:** Modest
**Address:** 11-12 Madeira Dr
Brighton BN2 1PS
**Phone:** +44 1273 604462

#220
**Pizza King**
**Cuisines:** Fast Food, Pizza
**Average price:** Modest
**Address:** 56 Preston Street
Brighton BN1 2HE
**Phone:** +44 1273 737272

#221
**Cafe Arcadia**
**Cuisines:** Coffee, Tea, Breakfast & Brunch
**Average price:** Inexpensive
**Address:** 7 Dyke Rd
Brighton BN1 3FE
**Phone:** +44 1273 326600

#222
**Swallow House**
**Cuisines:** Chinese, Fast Food
**Average price:** Inexpensive
**Address:** 3 Lewes Rd
Brighton BN2 3HP
**Phone:** +44 1273 692794

#223
**Pizza King**
**Cuisines:** Fast Food
**Average price:** Inexpensive
**Address:** 42 Kings Road
Brighton BN1 1NA
**Phone:** +44 1273 725225

#224
**Banjo's Sandwich Shop**
**Cuisines:** Coffee, Tea, Sandwiches,
Breakfast & Brunch
**Average price:** Inexpensive
**Address:** 9 Norfolk Sq
Brighton BN1 2PB
**Phone:** +44 1273 772836

#225
**China Town 2**
**Cuisines:** Fish & Chips, Fast Food, Chinese
**Average price:** Inexpensive
**Address:** 94 Upper Lewes Rd
Brighton BN2 3FE
**Phone:** +44 1273 380850

#226
**La Fourchette**
**Cuisines:** Coffee, Tea,
Breakfast & Brunch, French
**Average price:** Modest
**Address:** 42 Church Rd
Brighton BN3 2FN
**Phone:** +44 1273 733228

#227
**Lucky Voice Karaoke**
**Cuisines:** Karaoke, Bar, Pizza
**Average price:** Expensive
**Address:** 8 Black Lion Street
Brighton BN1 1ND
**Phone:** +44 1273 715770

#228
**All Bar One**
**Cuisines:** Wine Bar, British
**Average price:** Modest
**Address:** 2-3 Pavilion Bldg
Brighton BN1 1EE
**Phone:** +44 1273 207593

#229
**Day's Oriental Buffet**
**Cuisines:** Buffet, Asian Fusion
**Average price:** Modest
**Address:** 75 - 79 East St
Brighton BN1 1NF
**Phone:** +44 1273 748888

#230
**The Meeting Place**
**Cuisines:** Coffee, Tea, Breakfast & Brunch
**Average price:** Inexpensive
**Address:** Kings Road
Brighton BN1 2
**Phone:** +44 1273 206417

#231
**Sea Haze**
**Cuisines:** Seafood Market, Food Stand
**Average price:** Inexpensive
**Address:** 207 Kings Road
Brighton BN1 1NB
**Phone:** +44 1273 777007

#232
**Oxygen**
**Cuisines:** Lounge, Burgers
**Average price:** Inexpensive
**Address:** 74 West St
Brighton BN1 2RA
**Phone:** +44 1273 727378

#233
**Raj Pavillion**
**Cuisines:** Indian
**Average price:** Expensive
**Address:** 16 Preston Road
Brighton BN1 4QF
**Phone:** +44 1273 672255

#234
**Tookta's Cafe**
**Cuisines:** Thai
**Average price:** Modest
**Address:** 30 Spring St
Brighton BN1 3EF
**Phone:** +44 7881 854868

#235
**Iydea**
**Cuisines:** Vegetarian
**Average price:** Modest
**Address:** 105 Western Road
Brighton BN1 2AA
**Phone:** +44 1273 965904

#236
**Efes Kebab**
**Cuisines:** Fast Food
**Average price:** Inexpensive
**Address:** 53 Preston St
Brighton BN1 2HE
**Phone:** +44 1273 205133

#237
**Mr Noodles**
**Cuisines:** Japanese
**Average price:** Inexpensive
**Address:** 35 Queens Road
Brighton BN1 3XB
**Phone:** +44 1273 733999

#238
**Dig in the Ribs**
**Cuisines:** Tex-Mex, Mexican
**Average price:** Modest
**Address:** 47 Preston St
Brighton BN1 2HP
**Phone:** +44 1273 325275

#239
**Friends Fish & Chips**
**Cuisines:** Fish & Chips, Fast Food
**Average price:** Inexpensive
**Address:** 67 Queen's Rd
Brighton BN1 3XD
**Phone:** +44 1273 243665

#240
**Bella**
**Cuisines:** Italian, Coffee, Tea
**Average price:** Modest
**Address:** 120 St James St
Brighton BN2 1TH
**Phone:** +44 1273 623485

#241
**The Dip Cafe**
**Cuisines:** Coffee, Tea, Breakfast & Brunch
**Average price:** Modest
**Address:** 5 Hollingbury Place
Brighton BN1 7GE
**Phone:** +44 1273 563605

#242
**Street Thai**
**Cuisines:** Thai
**Average price:** Modest
**Address:** 20
Brighton Square
Brighton BN1 1HD
**Phone:** +44 1273 207444

#243
**Pause Cafe**
**Cuisines:** Coffee, Tea, Breakfast & Brunch
**Average price:** Modest
**Address:** 1 Circus Parade
Brighton BN1 4GW
**Phone:** +44 1273 690300

#244
**Thewitchez Photo Design Cafe Bar**
**Cuisines:** Café
**Average price:** Modest
**Address:** 16 Marine Parade
Brighton BN2 1TL
**Phone:** +44 1273 673652

#245
**Tortilla**
**Cuisines:** Mexican, Fast Food
**Average price:** Inexpensive
**Address:** 37 West Street
Brighton BN1 2RE
**Phone:** +44 1273 748069

#246
**Azure Restaurant**
**Cuisines:** Mediterranean,
Hookah Bar, Cocktail Bar
**Average price:** Modest
**Address:** 9-11 Lower Promenade
Brighton BN2 1PS
**Phone:** +44 1273 620856

#247
**The Blue Man**
**Cuisines:** African, Moroccan, Jazz, Blues
**Average price:** Modest
**Address:** 8 Queens Road
Brighton BN1 3WA
**Phone:** +44 1273 726003

#248
**GFC**
**Cuisines:** Fast Food
**Average price:** Modest
**Address:** 22 Church Rd
Brighton BN3 2FN
**Phone:** +44 1273 749490

#249
**Chez Dimitrina**
**Cuisines:** Coffee, Tea, French
**Average price:** Inexpensive
**Address:** 16 Sydney St
Brighton BN1 4EN
**Phone:** +44 1273 625222

#250
**Uncle Sams**
**Cuisines:** Burgers
**Average price:** Inexpensive
**Address:** 197 Carden Avenue
Brighton BN1 8LE
**Phone:** +44 1273 700748

#251
**The Brasserie Fish**
**Cuisines:** Seafood
**Average price:** Modest
**Address:** 3a Waterfront
Brighton BN2 5WA
**Phone:** +44 1273 698989

#252
**Lovefit Cafe**
**Cuisines:** Coffee, Tea,
Breakfast & Brunch, Juice Bar
**Average price:** Modest
**Address:** 110 Queens Road
Brighton BN1 3XF
**Phone:** +44 1273 720100

#253
**King & Queen**
**Cuisines:** Pub, British, Sports Bar
**Average price:** Inexpensive
**Address:** 13-17 Marlborough Place
Brighton BN1 1UB
**Phone:** +44 1273 607207

#254
**China Chef Express**
**Cuisines:** Chinese, Fast Food
**Average price:** Inexpensive
**Address:** 15 Beaconsfield Road
Brighton BN1 4QH
**Phone:** +44 1273 688290

#255
**Square Bar-Restaurant**
**Cuisines:** Wine Bar, Lounge, Italian
**Average price:** Modest
**Address:** 79 Western Road
Brighton BN3 2JQ
**Phone:** +44 1273 772777

#256
**China China**
**Cuisines:** Chinese
**Average price:** Inexpensive
**Address:** 33-35 Preston Street
Brighton BN1 2HP
**Phone:** +44 1273 328028

#257
**Pizza Express Restaurants**
**Cuisines:** Pizza
**Average price:** Modest
**Address:** 36 Ship Street
Brighton BN1 1AB
**Phone:** +44 1895 618618

#258
**Coffee Republic UK**
**Cuisines:** Coffee, Tea, Café
**Average price:** Expensive
**Address:** 54 Western Road
Brighton BN1 2EB
**Phone:** +44 1273 730550

#259
**The Office**
**Cuisines:** Pub, Thai
**Average price:** Expensive
**Address:** 8-9 Sydney Street
Brighton BN1 4EN
**Phone:** +44 1273 609134

#260
**Grubbs Diner**
**Cuisines:** Fast Food
**Average price:** Inexpensive
**Address:** 27 York Place
Brighton BN1 4GU
**Phone:** +44 1273 697226

#261
**Burger King**
**Cuisines:** American, Burgers, Fast Food
**Average price:** Inexpensive
**Address:** Madeira Drive
Brighton BN2 1TB
**Phone:** +44 1273 609029

#262
**Burger King**
**Cuisines:** American, Burgers, Fast Food
**Average price:** Inexpensive
**Address:** 63-65 North Street
Brighton BN1 1RH
**Phone:** +44 1273 325466

#263
**Tuckers**
**Cuisines:** Fast Food
**Average price:** Modest
**Address:** 100 ST. Georges Road
Brighton BN2 1EA
**Phone:** +44 1273 692452

#264
**Pomegranate**
**Cuisines:** Middle Eastern
**Average price:** Modest
**Address:** 10 Manchester Street
Brighton BN2 1TF
**Phone:** +44 1273 628386

#265
**Breakfast at Tiffany's**
**Cuisines:** Coffee, Tea,
Breakfast & Brunch, British
**Average price:** Inexpensive
**Address:** 22 North Rd
Brighton BN1 1YA
**Phone:** +44 1273 674209

#266
**Cafe All'Angolo**
**Cuisines:** Café, Breakfast & Brunch
**Average price:** Inexpensive
**Address:** 3-4 East Street
Brighton BN1 1HP
**Phone:** +44 1273 777312

#267
**Capers**
**Cuisines:** Coffee, Tea, British
**Average price:** Modest
**Address:** 27 Gardner Street
Brighton BN1 1UP
**Phone:** +44 1273 675550

#268
**LangeLee's**
**Cuisines:** Coffee, Tea, British
**Average price:** Modest
**Address:** 30 York Place
Brighton BN1 4
**Phone:** +44 1273 684840

#269
**Casa Della Pizza**
**Cuisines:** Italian
**Average price:** Inexpensive
**Address:** 27 North St
Brighton BN1 1EB
**Phone:** +44 1273 205441

#270
**Sushimania**
**Cuisines:** Japanese
**Average price:** Modest
**Address:** 15-17 Middle Street
Brighton BN1 1AL
**Phone:** +44 1273 324185

#271
**The Gourmet Fish
and Chip Company**
**Cuisines:** Coffee, Tea, Fish & Chips
**Average price:** Inexpensive
**Address:** 18 Waterfront
Brighton BN2 5WA
**Phone:** +44 1273 670701

#272
**The World's End**
**Cuisines:** Pub, Music Venues, Barbeque
**Average price:** Modest
**Address:** 60-61 London Road
Brighton BN1 4JE
**Phone:** +44 1273 692311

#273
**Destination 100**
**Cuisines:** Diner
**Average price:** Inexpensive
**Address:** 100 St. James St
Brighton BN2 1TP
**Phone:** +44 1273 606030

#274
**Pasha**
**Cuisines:** Seafood, Bar
**Average price:** Inexpensive
**Address:** 62 West Street
Brighton BN1 2RA
**Phone:** +44 1273 771010

#275
**The Eagle**
**Cuisines:** Pub, British
**Average price:** Modest
**Address:** 125 Gloucester Road
Brighton BN1 4AF
**Phone:** +44 1273 687185

#276
**Yummie Pizza**
**Cuisines:** Pizza, Fast Food
**Average price:** Inexpensive
**Address:** 3 Islingword Road
Brighton BN2 9SE
**Phone:** +44 1273 262728

#277
**La Florentina**
**Cuisines:** Italian, Portuguese
**Average price:** Modest
**Address:** 50 Norfolk Square
Brighton BN1 2PA
**Phone:** +44 1273 774049

#278
**The Gossip Cafe**
**Cuisines:** Diner
**Average price:** Modest
**Address:** 57 St James's St
Brighton BN2 1QG
**Phone:** +44 7796 867785

#279
**Sobs Takeaway**
**Cuisines:** Fast Food
**Average price:** Modest
**Address:** 16 Montpelier Place
Brighton BN1 3BF
**Phone:** +44 1273 729082

#280
**Papa John's Pizza
Brighton**
**Cuisines:** Pizza
**Average price:** Modest
**Address:** 13 Preston Road
Brighton BN1 4
**Phone:** +44 1273 607080

#281
**Las Tortas**
**Cuisines:** Italian
**Average price:** Inexpensive
**Address:** 48 Norfolk Square
Brighton BN1 2PA
**Phone:** +44 1273 737222

#282
**Rocky's**
**Cuisines:** Fast Food
**Average price:** Modest
**Address:** 147 Edward Street
Brighton BN2 0JG
**Phone:** +44 1273 687689

#283
**Caffe Nero**
**Cuisines:** Coffee, Tea, Sandwiches
**Average price:** Modest
**Address:** 16 Prince Albert St
Brighton BN1 1HF
**Phone:** +44 1273 727726

#284
**The Mash Tun**
**Cuisines:** Pub, British
**Average price:** Modest
**Address:** 1 Church Street
Brighton BN1 1UE
**Phone:** +44 1273 684951

#285
**Jenny's Fish & Chips**
**Cuisines:** Fish & Chips, Fast Food
**Average price:** Inexpensive
**Address:** 86 Preston Drove
Brighton BN1 6LB
**Phone:** +44 1273 881700

#286
**Cafe Motu**
**Cuisines:** Breakfast & Brunch, Coffee, Tea
**Average price:** Inexpensive
**Address:** 6 Trafalgar St
Brighton BN1 4EQ
**Phone:** +44 1273 709655

#287
**Anatolia Cuisine**
**Cuisines:** Caterer, Turkish
**Average price:** Inexpensive
**Address:** 51 St James Street
Brighton BN2 1QG
**Phone:** +44 1273 693467

#288
**The Creperie**
**Cuisines:** Crêperie
**Average price:** Inexpensive
**Address:** 2 Ship Street
Brighton BN1 1AD
**Phone:** +44 1273 323830

#289
**KFC**
**Cuisines:** Fast Food
**Average price:** Inexpensive
**Address:** 63-65 Western Road
Brighton BN1 2HA
**Phone:** +44 1273 328821

#290
**Loving Hut**
**Cuisines:** Vegan
**Average price:** Inexpensive
**Address:** The Level St Peter's Place
Brighton BN1 4SA
**Phone:** +44 1273 689532

#291
**Planet India**
**Cuisines:** Indian, Vegetarian, Fast Food
**Average price:** Modest
**Address:** 4 Richmond Parade
Brighton BN2 9PH
**Phone:** +44 1273 818149

#292
**Inside Out**
**Cuisines:** Coffee, Tea, Breakfast & Brunch
**Average price:** Modest
**Address:** 95 Gloucester Rd
Brighton BN1 4AP
**Phone:** +44 1273 692912

#293
**The Hampton**
**Cuisines:** Pub, Gastropub
**Average price:** Modest
**Address:** 57 Upper North St
Brighton BN1 3FH
**Phone:** +44 1273 731347

#294
**E-Kagen**
**Cuisines:** Japanese, Ethnic Food
**Average price:** Modest
**Address:** 5 Fenchurch Walk
Brighton BN1 4GX
**Phone:** +44 1273 819850

#295
**The Eddy**
**Cuisines:** Pub, British
**Average price:** Inexpensive
**Address:** 67a Upper Gloucester Road
Brighton BN1 3LQ
**Phone:** +44 1273 329540

#296
**Dover Castle**
**Cuisines:** Pub, Seafood
**Average price:** Expensive
**Address:** 43 Southover Street
Brighton BN2 9UE
**Phone:** +44 1273 245338

#297
**Delight Kebab**
**Cuisines:** Turkish
**Average price:** Expensive
**Address:** 15 Preston Road
Brighton BN1 4QE
**Phone:** +44 1273 695508

#298
**Katarina Harvester**
**Cuisines:** British, Pub
**Average price:** Modest
**Address:** Village Square
Brighton BN2 5WD
**Phone:** +44 1273 606268

#299
**Izzy Café**
**Cuisines:** Diner, Breakfast & Brunch
**Average price:** Inexpensive
**Address:** 2 St James's Street
Brighton BN1 1RE
**Phone:** +44 1273 660072

#300
**Neighbourhood**
**Cuisines:** Bar, Breakfast & Brunch, Café
**Average price:** Modest
**Address:** 101 Saint James Street
Brighton BN2 1TP
**Phone:** +44 1273 673891

#301
**Relax Cafe**
**Cuisines:** Coffee, Tea, Sandwiches
**Average price:** Inexpensive
**Address:** 50 Preston Road
Brighton BN1 4QF
**Phone:** +44 1273 818828

#302
**Model Fish Fryer**
**Cuisines:** Fish & Chips
**Average price:** Inexpensive
**Address:** 136 Preston Drove
Brighton BN1 6FJ
**Phone:** +44 1273 503871

#303
**Karma**
**Cuisines:** Pub, Restaurant
**Average price:** Modest
**Address:** 5 Waterfront
Brighton BN2 5WA
**Phone:** +44 1273 818000

#304
**La Capannina**
**Cuisines:** Italian
**Average price:** Modest
**Address:** 15 Madeira Place
Brighton BN2 1TN
**Phone:** +44 1273 680839

#305
**Sing-Li Fish Chips**
**Cuisines:** Seafood
**Average price:** Inexpensive
**Address:** 39 Guildford Road
Brighton BN1 3LW
**Phone:** +44 1273 328686

#306
**Costa Coffee**
**Cuisines:** Coffee, Tea,
Breakfast & Brunch, Sandwiches
**Average price:** Modest
**Address:** 17 London Road
Brighton BN1 4JA
**Phone:** +44 1273 604646

#307
**Yates**
**Cuisines:** Pub, Dance Club, British
**Average price:** Inexpensive
**Address:** 59 W Street
Brighton BN1 2RA
**Phone:** +44 1273 731117

#308
**Emporium**
**Cuisines:** Performing Arts, Café
**Average price:** Modest
**Address:** 88 London Road
Brighton BN1 4
**Phone:** +44 7530 636636

#309
**Strada -
Brighton Marina**
**Cuisines:** Italian
**Average price:** Expensive
**Address:** Brighton Marina
Brighton BN2 5WA
**Phone:** +44 1273 686821

#310
**The Cow**
**Cuisines:** Pub, British
**Average price:** Modest
**Address:** 95/97 Dyke Road
Brighton BN1 3JE
**Phone:** +44 1273 772370

#311
**Cummin Up**
**Cuisines:** Caribbean
**Average price:** Inexpensive
**Address:** 2 Preston Circus
Brighton BN1 4JQ
**Phone:** +44 1273 679000

#312
**Aroma Spice**
**Cuisines:** Indian, Fast Food
**Average price:** Inexpensive
**Address:** 4 Lewes Road
Brighton BN2 3HP
**Phone:** +44 1273 677608

#313
**Divalls Cafe**
**Cuisines:** Coffee, Tea, Breakfast & Brunch
**Average price:** Inexpensive
**Address:** 3 Terminus Road
Brighton BN1 3PD
**Phone:** +44 1273 776277

#314
**Costa Coffee**
**Cuisines:** Coffee, Tea, Sandwiches
**Average price:** Modest
**Address:** 2 Dyke Rd
Brighton BN1 3FE
**Phone:** +44 1273 725124

#315
**Joeies Takeaway**
**Cuisines:** Pizza, Fast Food
**Average price:** Inexpensive
**Address:** 32 Viaduct Rd
Brighton BN1 4NB
**Phone:** +44 1273 708080

#316
**The Prince Arthur**
**Cuisines:** Pub, British
**Average price:** Modest
**Address:** 38 Dean Street
Brighton BN1 3EG
**Phone:** +44 1273 205797

#317
**Smoque Grill**
**Cuisines:** Burgers
**Average price:** Inexpensive
**Address:** 76 Islingword Road
Brighton BN2 9SL
**Phone:** +44 1273 684681

#318
**Pizza Hut**
**Cuisines:** Pizza, Fast Food
**Average price:** Modest
**Address:** 132 - 135 Lewes Rd
Brighton BN2 3LG
**Phone:** +44 1273 670670

#319
**Indian Summer**
**Cuisines:** Indian
**Average price:** Expensive
**Address:** 69 E Street
Brighton BN1 1HQ
**Phone:** +44 1273 711001

#320
**Brighton Wok**
**Cuisines:** Fast Food, Chinese
**Average price:** Modest
**Address:** 34 New England Road
Brighton BN1 4GG
**Phone:** +44 1273 270490

#321
**Golden Grill**
**Cuisines:** Fast Food
**Average price:** Inexpensive
**Address:** 7 Station Road
Brighton BN41 1GA
**Phone:** +44 1273 417414

#322
**Hasina Tandoori**
**Cuisines:** Fast Food
**Average price:** Modest
**Address:** 92 Preston Drove
Brighton BN1 6LB
**Phone:** +44 1273 542626

#323
**China Garden Restaurant**
**Cuisines:** Dim Sum
**Average price:** Modest
**Address:** 88-91 Preston Street
Brighton BN1 2HG
**Phone:** +44 1273 325124

#324
**Marions**
**Cuisines:** Coffee, Tea,
Breakfast & Brunch, British
**Average price:** Modest
**Address:** 3 Beaconsfield Parade
Brighton BN1 6DN
**Phone:** +44 1273 556526

#325
**Pret a Manger**
**Cuisines:** Coffee, Tea, Sandwiches
**Average price:** Inexpensive
**Address:** 35 East St
Brighton BN1 1HL
**Phone:** +44 20 7932 5397

#326
**Out To Lunch**
**Cuisines:** Fast Food, Sandwiches
**Average price:** Inexpensive
**Address:** 8 Preston Road
Brighton BN1 4QF
**Phone:** +44 1273 694390

#327
**Green Tomato**
**Cuisines:** Coffee, Tea, Sandwiches
**Average price:** Modest
**Address:** 100a Western Rd
Brighton BN1 2AA
**Phone:** +44 1273 727285

#328
**Pizzaiola Pizza**
**Cuisines:** Pizza
**Average price:** Inexpensive
**Address:** 76 Islingword Road
Brighton BN2 9SL
**Phone:** +44 1273 684681

#329
**Lodestar Cafe**
**Cuisines:** Sandwiches, Breakfast & Brunch
**Average price:** Modest
**Address:** 163 Kings Road Arches
Brighton BN1 1NB
**Phone:** +44 7973 296514

#330
**Cafe Laziz**
**Cuisines:** Coffee, Tea, British, Sandwiches
**Average price:** Modest
**Address:** 48 Gardner Street
Brighton BN1 1UN
**Phone:** +44 1273 625544

#331
**Master Mariner**
**Cuisines:** Pub, British
**Average price:** Modest
**Address:** Village Square
Brighton BN2 5WD
**Phone:** +44 1273 818563

#332
**Pizza Hut**
**Cuisines:** Pizza, Fast Food
**Average price:** Modest
**Address:** 2 Dyke Road
Brighton BN1 3FE
**Phone:** +44 1273 328666

#333
**Mac's Cafe**
**Cuisines:** Coffee, Tea,
Breakfast & Brunch, British
**Average price:** Modest
**Address:** 30 Arundel Road
Brighton BN2 5TD
**Phone:** +44 1273 692621

#334
**McDonald's**
**Cuisines:** Fast Food
**Average price:** Inexpensive
**Address:** Unit A Churchill Square
Brighton BN1 2TE
**Phone:** +44 1273 747924

#335
**China Kitchen**
**Cuisines:** Fast Food
**Average price:** Inexpensive
**Address:** 17 Coombe Terrace Lewes Road
Brighton BN2 4AD
**Phone:** +44 1273 680894

#336
**Kebab Knight**
**Cuisines:** Fast Food
**Average price:** Modest
**Address:** 15 Coombe Terrace
Brighton BN2 4AD
**Phone:** +44 1273 690771

#337
**Grand Central**
**Cuisines:** Pub, Gastropub
**Average price:** Modest
**Address:** 29-30 Surrey Street
Brighton BN1 3PA
**Phone:** +44 1273 329086

#338
**Athena B Fish Bar**
**Cuisines:** Fish & Chips
**Average price:** Modest
**Address:** 27 Station Rd
Brighton BN41 1DF
**Phone:** +44 1273 414803

#339
**Donatello Restaurant**
**Cuisines:** Italian, Pizza
**Average price:** Modest
**Address:** 1-3
Brighton Place
Brighton BN1 1HJ
**Phone:** +44 1273 775477

#340
**Sichuan Garden**
**Cuisines:** Fast Food
**Average price:** Inexpensive
**Address:** 58 Queens Road
Brighton BN1 3XD
**Phone:** +44 1273 324767

#341
**Cous Cous House**
**Cuisines:** Moroccan, Persian, Iranian
**Average price:** Modest
**Address:** 10-11 Preston Street
Brighton BN1 2HN
**Phone:** +44 1273 323230

#342
**The Swan**
**Cuisines:** British
**Average price:** Expensive
**Address:** No 9 Rock St
Brighton BN2 1NF
**Phone:** +44 1273 606138

#343
**Infinity Foods Kitchen**
**Cuisines:** Coffee, Tea,
Vegetarian, Breakfast & Brunch
**Average price:** Modest
**Address:** 50 Gardner Street
Brighton BN1 1UN
**Phone:** +44 1273 670743

#344
**Piccolo**
**Cuisines:** Italian
**Average price:** Inexpensive
**Address:** 56 Ship Street
Brighton BN1 1AF
**Phone:** +44 4412 7338 0380

#345
**P C Pickles**
**Cuisines:** Fast Food
**Average price:** Inexpensive
**Address:** 3-6 Francis Street
Brighton BN1 4JT
**Phone:** +44 1273 622113

#346
**The Iron Duke**
**Cuisines:** Pub, Guest Houses, British
**Average price:** Modest
**Address:** 3 Waterloo Street
Brighton BN3 1AQ
**Phone:** +44 1273 734806

#347
**Curry Hut**
**Cuisines:** Fast Food, Indian
**Average price:** Inexpensive
**Address:** 162 Edward Street
Brighton BN2 0JB
**Phone:** +44 1273 609349

#348
**Palm Court**
**Cuisines:** British
**Average price:** Expensive
**Address:** Madeira Drive
Brighton BN2 1TW
**Phone:** +44 872 148 6077

#349
**Poppy's Sandwich Bar**
**Cuisines:** Coffee, Tea, Sandwiches
**Average price:** Inexpensive
**Address:** 58a London Road
Brighton BN1 4JE
**Phone:** +44 1273 672235

#350
**Wetherspoons**
**Cuisines:** Pub, British
**Average price:** Inexpensive
**Address:** 20-22a West Street
Brighton BN1 2RE
**Phone:** +44 1273 224690

#351
**Italian Delicatessen**
**Cuisines:** Deli, Coffee, Tea, Delicatessen
**Average price:** Modest
**Address:** 92 Dyke Road
Brighton BN1 3JD
**Phone:** +44 1273 326147

#352
**Terraces Bar and Grill**
**Cuisines:** Restaurant
**Average price:** Modest
**Address:** Marine Parade
Brighton BN2
**Phone:** +44 1273 570526

#353
**Wokmania**
**Cuisines:** Chinese, Vegetarian
**Average price:** Expensive
**Address:** Unit 1 Avalon 65 West Street
Brighton BN1 2RA
**Phone:** +44 1273 746294

#354
**Dial A Pizza**
**Cuisines:** Fast Food, Convenience Store
**Average price:** Modest
**Address:** 103 Dyke Road
Brighton BN1 3JE
**Phone:** +44 1273 220021

#355
**Subway**
**Cuisines:** Sandwiches
**Average price:** Inexpensive
**Address:** 109 Queens Road
Brighton BN1 3XF
**Phone:** +44 1273 722333

#356
**Goemon Ramen Bar**
**Cuisines:** Ramen
**Average price:** Inexpensive
**Address:** 12 Preston Street
Brighton BN1 2HN
**Phone:** +44 1273 241226

#357
**Our Cornish Pasty Shop**
**Cuisines:** Bakery, Desserts, Fast Food
**Average price:** Inexpensive
**Address:** 24 Gardner Street
Brighton BN1 1UP
**Phone:** +44 1273 688063

#358
**The French Revolution: Coffee Workshop Creperie**
**Cuisines:** Crêperie, Coffee, Tea
**Average price:** Inexpensive
**Address:** Engineering 2 / The Richmond Building Brighton BN1 9QT
**Phone:** +44 1273 877205

#359
**Dos Sombreros**
**Cuisines:** Mexican
**Average price:** Modest
**Address:** 24 Ship Street
Brighton BN1 1AD
**Phone:** +44 1273 911455

#360
**Kemp Town Chippy**
**Cuisines:** Fish & Chips
**Average price:** Inexpensive
**Address:** 73 ST Georges Road
Brighton BN2 1EF
**Phone:** +44 1273 680821

#361
**Akash Tandoori**
**Cuisines:** Indian, Pakistani
**Average price:** Modest
**Address:** 26 Preston Street
Brighton BN1 2HN
**Phone:** +44 1273 820213

#362
**Strada Restaurants**
**Cuisines:** Italian
**Average price:** Modest
**Address:** 3 Waterfront
Brighton BN2 5WA
**Phone:** +44 1273 686821

#363
**Sa Sa Fish & Chips**
**Cuisines:** Fish & Chips
**Average price:** Inexpensive
**Address:** 20 Coombe Terrace
Brighton BN2 4AD
**Phone:** +44 1273 570658

#364
**The Plaza**
**Cuisines:** Italian
**Average price:** Modest
**Address:** 43-45 Kings Road
Brighton BN1 1NA
**Phone:** +44 1273 232222

#365
**Cowley Club**
**Cuisines:** Health Market,
Music Venues, Vegan
**Average price:** Modest
**Address:** 12 London Road
Brighton BN1 4JA
**Phone:** +44 872 148 6259

#366
**Bellota Bar Y Tapas**
**Cuisines:** Spanish, Tapas Bar
**Average price:** Modest
**Address:** 165 North Street
Brighton BN1 1EA
**Phone:** +44 1273 737342

#367
**The courtyard**
**Cuisines:** Restaurant
**Average price:** Modest
**Address:** 20 New road
Brighton BN1
**Phone:** +44 1273 819600

#368
**The Trawlerman**
**Cuisines:** Fish & Chips
**Average price:** Inexpensive
**Address:** 106 Gloucester Road
Brighton BN1 4AP
**Phone:** +44 1273 681601

#369
**Bengal Cuisine**
**Cuisines:** Fast Food, Indian
**Average price:** Modest
**Address:** 4 Loyal Parade
Brighton BN1 5GG
**Phone:** +44 1273 565545

#370
**The Gossip Cafe**
**Cuisines:** Diner, Coffee, Tea
**Average price:** Inexpensive
**Address:** 54 Station Road
Brighton BN3 3
**Phone:** +44 1273 411901

#371
**Utopia Cafe**
**Cuisines:** Coffee, Tea, Café
**Average price:** Modest
**Address:** 49 Gardner St
Brighton BN1 1UN
**Phone:** +44 1273 818844

#372
**Lee's Garden**
**Cuisines:** Fast Food, Chinese
**Average price:** Inexpensive
**Address:** 186 Lewes Road
Brighton BN2 3LD
**Phone:** +44 1273 600138

#373
**Maharani Indian Takeaway**
**Cuisines:** Fast Food
**Average price:** Modest
**Address:** 52 Sillwood Street
Brighton BN1 2PS
**Phone:** +44 1273 748001

#374
**KFC**
**Cuisines:** Fast Food
**Average price:** Modest
**Address:** 22-23 London Road
Brighton BN1 4JB
**Phone:** +44 1273 691598

#375
**Sobs**
**Cuisines:** Fast Food, Turkish
**Average price:** Modest
**Address:** 3 Islingword Road
Brighton BN2 9SE
**Phone:** +44 1273 700088

#376
**Golden Fry**
**Cuisines:** Fast Food, Fish & Chips
**Average price:** Inexpensive
**Address:** 2 Parade Valley Drive
Brighton BN1 5FG
**Phone:** +44 1273 501444

#377
**Jalalia Tandoori Takeaway**
**Cuisines:** Indian
**Average price:** Inexpensive
**Address:** 31 Baker Street
Brighton BN1 4JN
**Phone:** +44 1273 682288

#378
**Real Patisserie**
**Cuisines:** Patisserie/Cake Shop, Bakery
**Average price:** Inexpensive
**Address:** 34 St George's Road
Brighton BN2 1ED
**Phone:** +44 1273 609655

#379
**Smugglers Restaurant**
**Cuisines:** Fish & Chips, Fast Food
**Average price:** Modest
**Address:** 36 High Street
Brighton BN2 7HR
**Phone:** +44 1273 309477

#380
**Park Crescent**
**Cuisines:** Pub, British
**Average price:** Modest
**Address:** 39 Park Crescent Terrace
Brighton BN2 3HE
**Phone:** +44 1273 604993

#381
**Cheeky Chicken**
**Cuisines:** Fast Food
**Average price:** Inexpensive
**Address:** 59 Preston Street
Brighton BN1 2HE
**Phone:** +44 1273 822888

#382
**The Romans pub**
**Cuisines:** Pub, Venues, Event Space
**Average price:** Modest
**Address:** Manor Hall road
Brighton BN42
**Phone:** +44 1273 592147

#383
**Seven Bees Cafe**
**Cuisines:** Coffee, Tea, Local Flavor,
Breakfast & Brunch
**Average price:** Inexpensive
**Address:** 7b Ship Street Gardens
Brighton BN2 1ED
**Phone:** +44 1273 279448

#384
**White Horse Hotel**
**Cuisines:** Hotel, Restaurant
**Average price:** Inexpensive
**Address:** Marine Drive
Brighton BN2 7HR
**Phone:** +44 1273 300301

#385
**The Devil's Dyke Inn**
**Cuisines:** Brasseries, Beer, Wine, Spirits,
British, Local Flavor, Landmark/Historical
**Average price:** Modest
**Address:** Dyke Road
Brighton BN1 8YJ
**Phone:** +44 1273 857256

#386
**Yo Sushi**
**Cuisines:** Sushi Bar
**Average price:** Modest
**Address:** 6 Jubilee St
Brighton BN1 1GE
**Phone:** +44 1273 689659

#387
**The Old Cottage
Tea Rooms & Restaurant**
**Cuisines:** Coffee, Tea, British
**Average price:** Modest
**Address:** 62-64 High Street
Brighton BN2 7HF
**Phone:** +44 1273 303426

#388
**El Taco**
**Cuisines:** Tex-Mex, Mexican
**Average price:** Inexpensive
**Address:** 100 Western Road
Brighton BN1 2AA
**Phone:** +44 1273 725861

#389
**The Cricketers**
**Cuisines:** Pub, British
**Average price:** Modest
**Address:** 15 Black Lion Street
Brighton BN1 1ND
**Phone:** +44 1273 329472

#390
**Los Amigos**
**Cuisines:** Mexican, Tex-Mex
**Average price:** Expensive
**Address:** 60 Church Road Hove BN3 2FP
**Phone:** +44 1273 778777

#391
**Piazza**
**Cuisines:** Pizza, Burgers
**Average price:** Modest
**Address:** 542 Falmer Road
Brighton BN2 6ND
**Phone:** +44 1273 300011

#392
**Sichuan Chef**
**Cuisines:** Chinese
**Average price:** Modest
**Address:** 18-19 York Place
Brighton BN1 4GU
**Phone:** +44 1273 698606

#393
**Frankie Vaughns**
**Cuisines:** Sandwiches, Coffee, Tea
**Average price:** Expensive
**Address:** 180 Edward Street
Brighton BN2 0JB
**Phone:** +44 1273 818888

#394
**Carats Cafe Bar**
**Cuisines:** Coffee, Tea,
Breakfast & Brunch, Café
**Average price:** Modest
**Address:** Southwick Beach
Brighton BN41 1WD
**Phone:** +44 1273 430924

#395
**Wai Kika Moo Kau**
**Cuisines:** Vegetarian, Vegan, Café
**Average price:** Modest
**Address:** 11a Kensington Gardens
Brighton BN1 4AL
**Phone:** +44 1273 671117

#396
**Western Front**
**Cuisines:** Pub, Social Club, British
**Average price:** Inexpensive
**Address:** 11 Cranbourne St
Brighton BN1 2RD
**Phone:** +44 1273 725656

#397
**Tutti Frutti**
**Cuisines:** Food, Italian
**Average price:** Modest
**Address:** 92 Dyke Rd
Brighton BN1 3DJ
**Phone:** +44 1273 326147

#398
**Choices**
**Cuisines:** Fast Food
**Average price:** Inexpensive
**Address:** 98 Valley Road
Brighton BN41 2TL
**Phone:** +44 1273 420620

#399
**Kemp Spices**
**Cuisines:** Indian, Pakistani, Fast Food
**Average price:** Modest
**Address:** 51 St Georges Road
Brighton BN2 1EF
**Phone:** +44 1273 623331

#400
**Al Duomo**
**Cuisines:** Italian, Pizza, Coffee, Tea
**Average price:** Expensive
**Address:** 7 Pavilion Buildings
Brighton BN1 1EE
**Phone:** +44 1273 326741

#401
**The Empire Tandoori**
**Cuisines:** Fast Food, Indian
**Average price:** Modest
**Address:** 76 Lewes Road
Brighton BN2 3HZ
**Phone:** +44 1273 687400

#402
**Bombay Aloo Mix**
**Cuisines:** Indian, Pakistani
**Average price:** Inexpensive
**Address:** 119 St James's Street
Brighton BN2 1TH
**Phone:** +44 1273 622133

#403
**Terraces**
**Cuisines:** American
**Average price:** Modest
**Address:** Madeira Dr
Brighton BN2 1PS
**Phone:** +44 1273 545250

#404
**Spice Nutriment**
**Cuisines:** Indian, Fast Food
**Average price:** Modest
**Address:** 66 Queens Road
Brighton BN1 3XD
**Phone:** +44 1273 777746

#405
**Um Elnour**
**Cuisines:** Fast Food
**Average price:** Inexpensive
**Address:** 16 Western Road
Brighton BN3
**Phone:** +44 1273 771478

#406
**Fat Leo**
**Cuisines:** Italian, Pizza
**Average price:** Modest
**Address:** 16 Market Street
Brighton BN1 1HH
**Phone:** +44 1273 325135

#407
**Vineyard Steak House**
**Cuisines:** Greek, Mediterranean
**Average price:** Expensive
**Address:** 64 Preston Street
Brighton BN1 2HE
**Phone:** +44 1273 321681

#408
**Café Delice**
**Cuisines:** Breakfast & Brunch,
Café, Brasseries
**Average price:** Modest
**Address:** 40 Kensignton Gardens
Brighton BN1 4AL
**Phone:** +44 1273 622519

#409
**Pizza Di Roma**
**Cuisines:** Fast Food, Halal
**Average price:** Inexpensive
**Address:** 51 Lewes Road
Brighton BN2 3HW
**Phone:** +44 1273 626233

#410
**Noori's**
**Cuisines:** Indian
**Average price:** Modest
**Address:** 70-71 Ship Street
Brighton BN1 1AE
**Phone:** +44 1273 747109

#411
**Hove Tandoori**
**Cuisines:** Indian, Pakistani
**Average price:** Modest
**Address:** 175 Church Road
Hove BN3 2AB
**Phone:** +44 1273 737188

#412
**Sukhothai Palace**
**Cuisines:** Thai
**Average price:** Modest
**Address:** 62 Middle St
Brighton BN1 1AL
**Phone:** +44 1273 748448

#413
**Otello Cafe**
**Cuisines:** Coffee, Tea, Italian
**Average price:** Modest
**Address:** 120 Church Rd
Brighton BN3 2AE
**Phone:** +44 1273 729774

#414
**Graze Restaurant**
**Cuisines:** British, Tapas
**Average price:** Expensive
**Address:** 42 Western Road Hove BN3 1JD
**Phone:** +44 1273 823707

#415
**Buon Appetito**
**Cuisines:** Italian, Pizza
**Average price:** Modest
**Address:** 81 Western Road
Hove BN3 2JQ
**Phone:** +44 1273 204848

#416
**Sabai**
**Cuisines:** Thai
**Average price:** Modest
**Address:** 165-169 Princes House
Brighton BN1 1EA
**Phone:** +44 1273 773030

#417
**Anna's Cafe**
**Cuisines:** Coffee, Tea, Breakfast & Brunch
**Average price:** Inexpensive
**Address:** 3 North Street
Brighton BN41 1DH
**Phone:** +44 1273 888222

#418
**Bangkok Express**
**Cuisines:** Fast Food, Thai
**Average price:** Modest
**Address:** 81 London Road
Brighton BN1 4JF
**Phone:** +44 1273 696816

#419
**Phoenix Palace**
**Cuisines:** Chinese, Fast Food
**Average price:** Inexpensive
**Address:** 35 Boundary Rd
Brighton BN3 4EF
**Phone:** +44 1273 417469

#420
**VBites**
**Cuisines:** Vegan
**Average price:** Modest
**Address:** Hove Lagoon
Brighton BN3 4LX
**Phone:** +44 1273 933757

#421
**Zafferelli**
**Cuisines:** Italian, Pizza
**Average price:** Inexpensive
**Address:** 31-32 New Road
Brighton BN1 1UG
**Phone:** +44 1273 206662

#422
**Subway**
**Cuisines:** Sandwiches
**Average price:** Inexpensive
**Address:** 134 London Road
Brighton BN1 4JH
**Phone:** +44 1273 628941

#423
**Eshnas Nutrition Indian Takeaway**
**Cuisines:** Fast Food, Indian
**Average price:** Modest
**Address:** 4 Coombe Terrace
Brighton BN2 4AD
**Phone:** +44 1273 570606

#424
**Dave's Diner**
**Cuisines:** Coffee, Tea, British
**Average price:** Inexpensive
**Address:** 87 Lewes Road
Brighton BN2 3HZ
**Phone:** +44 1273 697696

#425
**Valley Wok**
**Cuisines:** Fast Food
**Average price:** Inexpensive
**Address:** 104 Valley Road
Brighton BN41 2TL
**Phone:** +44 1273 888262

#426
**Fraser's Sandwich Station**
**Cuisines:** Coffee, Tea,
Sandwiches, Fast Food
**Average price:** Inexpensive
**Address:** 1A Castle Sq
Brighton BN1 1EG
**Phone:** +44 1273 202067

#427
**Rajah**
**Cuisines:** Indian
**Average price:** Modest
**Address:** 163 Old Shoreham Road
Brighton BN42 4QB
**Phone:** +44 1273 593636

#428
**Giraffe**
**Cuisines:** American
**Average price:** Modest
**Address:** Jubilee St
Brighton BN1 1GE
**Phone:** +44 1273 688885

#429
**Sami Swoi**
**Cuisines:** Polish
**Average price:** Modest
**Address:** 71 Boundary Road
Brighton BN3 5TD
**Phone:** +44 1273 420616

#430
**Tandoori Bites**
**Cuisines:** Indian, Fast Food
**Average price:** Modest
**Address:** 5 Victoria Terrace
Brighton BN3 2WB
**Phone:** +44 1273 773090

#431
**La Tasca**
**Cuisines:** Spanish, Basque
**Average price:** Expensive
**Address:** 165 North Street
Brighton BN1 1EA
**Phone:** +44 1273 737342

#432
**Dilshad Tandoori**
**Cuisines:** Fast Food, Indian
**Average price:** Modest
**Address:** 366 Mile Oak Road
Brighton BN41 2RA
**Phone:** +44 1273 415282

#433
**The White Rabbit**
**Cuisines:** Pub, British, Gastropub
**Average price:** Expensive
**Address:** 13 Kensington Gardens
Brighton BN1 4AL
**Phone:** +44 1273 677655

#434
**Topolino's Duo**
**Cuisines:** Italian
**Average price:** Modest
**Address:** 67 Church Road
Hove BN3 2BD
**Phone:** +44 1273 725726

#435
**All Nite Diner**
**Cuisines:** Diner
**Average price:** Expensive
**Address:** 19-21 Market Street
Brighton BN2 9QF
**Phone:** +44 1273 608273

#436
**The Hove Kitchen**
**Cuisines:** Pub, British, European
**Average price:** Modest
**Address:** 102-105 Western Road
Hove BN3 1FA
**Phone:** +44 1273 725495

#437
**The Giggling Squid**
**Cuisines:** Thai, Tapas, Seafood
**Average price:** Modest
**Address:** 129 Church Road
Hove BN3 2AE
**Phone:** +44 1273 771991

#438
**Aristocrats**
**Cuisines:** Gastropub
**Average price:** Inexpensive
**Address:** 54 Preston St
Brighton BN1 2HE
**Phone:** +44 1273 748388

#439
**The Connaught**
**Cuisines:** Gastropub, British
**Average price:** Modest
**Address:** 48 Hove Street
Hove BN3 2DH
**Phone:** +44 1273 206578

#440
**Hove Park Deli**
**Cuisines:** Deli, Caterer
**Average price:** Expensive
**Address:** 73 Old Shoreham Road
Hove BN3 7BE
**Phone:** +44 1273 777779

#441
**Marrocco's**
**Cuisines:** Italian
**Average price:** Modest
**Address:** 8 Kings Esplanade
Hove BN3 2WA
**Phone:** +44 1273 203764

#442
**The View**
**Cuisines:** European, Seafood
**Average price:** Modest
**Address:** Western Esplanade Kingsway
Brighton BN3 4FA
**Phone:** +44 1273 207100

#443
**Memories Of India**
**Cuisines:** Indian, Pakistani
**Average price:** Modest
**Address:** 9b Waterfront
Brighton BN2 5WA
**Phone:** +44 1273 600088

#444
**24 St Georges Restaurant**
**Cuisines:** European
**Average price:** Expensive
**Address:** 24-25 St Georges Rd
Brighton BN2 1ED
**Phone:** +44 1273 626060

#445
**The Green Mango**
**Cuisines:** Thai
**Average price:** Expensive
**Address:** 8 Church Rd Hove BN3 2
**Phone:** +44 1273 327226

#446
**Shake & Burger**
**Cuisines:** Fast Food
**Average price:** Inexpensive
**Address:** 37 Albion Street
Brighton BN42 4DN
**Phone:** +44 1273 706006

#447
**Thai Orchid**
**Cuisines:** Thai
**Average price:** Modest
**Address:** 65 Preston St
Brighton BN1 2HE
**Phone:** +44 1273 323224

#448
**Kemp Town Deli**
**Cuisines:** Deli, Coffee, Tea
**Average price:** Expensive
**Address:** 108 St Georges Rd
Brighton BN2 1EA
**Phone:** +44 1273 603411

#449
**The Dugout**
**Cuisines:** Pizza, Sports Bar
**Average price:** Modest
**Address:** 106 Lewes Road
Brighton BN2 3QA
**Phone:** +44 1273 622310

#450
**Bombay Lounge**
**Cuisines:** Indian, Pakistani
**Average price:** Inexpensive
**Address:** 30-31 North Street
Brighton BN1 1EB
**Phone:** +44 1273 777355

#451
**Balti Express**
**Cuisines:** Fast Food
**Average price:** Inexpensive
**Address:** 72 Beaconsfield Road
Brighton BN1 6DD
**Phone:** +44 1273 562228

#452
**Namul**
**Cuisines:** Korean
**Average price:** Inexpensive
**Address:** 49 Gardner Street
The Lanes BN1 1UN
**Phone:** +44 1273 973878

#453
**Saffrons**
**Cuisines:** Indian, Fast Food
**Average price:** Modest
**Address:** 2 Coombe Ter
East Sussex BN2 4AD
**Phone:** +44 1273 681280

#454
**Makara**
**Cuisines:** Turkish, Halal
**Average price:** Modest
**Address:** 28 Church Road
Hove BN3 2FN
**Phone:** +44 1273 748072

#455
**Grubbs Burgers**
**Cuisines:** Fast Food
**Average price:** Inexpensive
**Address:** 62 Western Rd
Hove BN3 1JD
**Phone:** +44 1273 736526

#456
**Hove Park**
**Cuisines:** Café
**Average price:** Inexpensive
**Address:** Parkview Road
Hove BN3 7BF
**Phone:** +44 1273 293080

#457
**Woodies Longboard Diner**
**Cuisines:** Burgers, Diner
**Average price:** Modest
**Address:** 366 Kingsway
Hove BN3 4QT
**Phone:** +44 1273 430300

#458
**Mile Oak Fisheries**
**Cuisines:** Fast Food
**Average price:** Inexpensive
**Address:** 364 Mile Oak Road
Brighton BN41 2RA
**Phone:** +44 1273 415794

#459
**Mykonos Greek Taverna**
**Cuisines:** Greek
**Average price:** Modest
**Address:** 31 Preston Street
Brighton BN1 2HP
**Phone:** +44 1273 329918

#460
**Le Gourmet**
**Cuisines:** Deli, Coffee, Tea
**Average price:** Exclusive
**Address:** 159 Dyke Road
Hove BN3 1TJ
**Phone:** +44 1273 778437

#461
**Riddle & Finns II**
**Cuisines:** Seafood
**Average price:** Expensive
**Address:** 139 Kings Road Arches
The City of Brighton and Hove BN1 2FN
**Phone:** +44 1273 821218

#462
**The Garden Cafe**
**Cuisines:** Coffee, Tea, British
**Average price:** Inexpensive
**Address:** St Anns Well Gardens
Brighton and Hove BN3 1RP
**Phone:** +44 1273 735187

#463
**Otello Restaurant**
**Cuisines:** Italian
**Average price:** Modest
**Address:** 122 Church Road
Hove BN3 2EA
**Phone:** +44 1273 227173

#464
**Frankie & Benny's**
**Cuisines:** Italian
**Average price:** Modest
**Address:** Unit 3 Waterfront
Brighton BN2 5WA
**Phone:** +44 1273 688450

#465
**Smokeys**
**Brighton**
**Cuisines:** Barbeque
**Average price:** Modest
**Address:** 124 Kings Road
The City of Brighton and Hove BN1 2FA
**Phone:** +44 1273 323888

#466
**Rotunda Cafe**
**Cuisines:** Coffee, Tea, Desserts, Sandwiches
**Average price:** Modest
**Address:** 10-11 Preston Street
Brighton BN1 6HN
**Phone:** +44 1273 555460

#467
**Happy Garden**
**Cuisines:** Chinese
**Average price:** Inexpensive
**Address:** 15 Western Road
Brighton BN3 1AE
**Phone:** +44 1273 738009

#468
**Thai Connection Catering**
**Cuisines:** Thai, Fast Food
**Average price:** Modest
**Address:** 14 Blatchington Road
Hove BN3 3YN
**Phone:** +44 1273 205009

#469
**Figaro's**
**Cuisines:** Breakfast & Brunch,
British, Sandwiches
**Average price:** Inexpensive
**Address:** 13 George St
Brighton BN2 1RH
**Phone:** +44 1273 688811

#470
**Caffe Bar Italia**
**Cuisines:** Café
**Average price:** Modest
**Address:** 24 George Street
Hove BN3 3YA
**Phone:** +44 7801 098608

#471
**The Bell**
**Cuisines:** Pub, British
**Average price:** Modest
**Address:** 15-17 Belfast Street
Hove BN3 3YS
**Phone:** +44 1273 770773

#472
**64 Degrees**
**Cuisines:** Tapas
**Average price:** Expensive
**Address:** 53 Meeting House Lane
Brighton BN1 1HB
**Phone:** +44 1273 770115

#473
**Crêperie Angélie**
**Cuisines:** Crêperie
**Average price:** Inexpensive
**Address:** 9 Duke Street
Brighton BN1 1AH
**Phone:** +44 1273 325433

#474
**Galileo Pizzeria**
**Cuisines:** Italian, Pizza
**Average price:** Modest
**Address:** 1 Woodland Parade
Hove BN3 6DR
**Phone:** +44 1273 330883

#475
**A'Maze Oriental**
**Cuisines:** Malaysian, Thai, Japanese
**Average price:** Modest
**Address:** 73a Western Road
Brighton BN1 2
**Phone:** +44 1273 205777

#476
**Kenzi**
**Cuisines:** Irish, Moroccan
**Average price:** Modest
**Address:** 42 Church Road
Hove BN3 2FN
**Phone:** +44 1273 733228

#477
**Eat**
**Cuisines:** Coffee, Tea, Café
**Average price:** Inexpensive
**Address:** Churchill Square
Brighton and Hove BN1 2RG
**Phone:** +44 1273 732380

#478
**Latino Restaurant**
**Cuisines:** Spanish, Cocktail Bar, Tapas Bar
**Average price:** Modest
**Address:** 36 Church Road
Hove BN3 2FN
**Phone:** +44 1273 770355

#479
**Indiana Restaurant**
**Cuisines:** Indian, Pakistani
**Average price:** Modest
**Address:** 4 Church Road
Hove BN3 2FL
**Phone:** +44 1273 731354

#480
**Orsino Restaurant**
**Cuisines:** Italian, Steakhouse, Seafood
**Average price:** Modest
**Address:** 141 Church Road
Hove BN3 2AE
**Phone:** +44 1273 770999

#481
**Caroline Of Brunswick**
**Cuisines:** Pub, British
**Average price:** Inexpensive
**Address:** 39 Ditchling Road
Brighton BN1 4SB
**Phone:** +44 1273 624434

#482
**Burger Off**
**Cuisines:** Fast Food, Burgers
**Average price:** Inexpensive
**Address:** 52 Brunswick St
West Hove BN3 1EL
**Phone:** +44 1273 326655

#483
**Sahara**
**Cuisines:** Middle Eastern
**Average price:** Modest
**Address:** 103 Western Road
Brighton BN1 2AA
**Phone:** +44 1273 730123

#484
**Leonardo Ristorante Italiano**
**Cuisines:** Italian
**Average price:** Inexpensive
**Address:** 55 Church Road
Hove BN3 2BD
**Phone:** +44 1273 328888

#485
**Bali Brasserie**
**Cuisines:** Restaurant, Bar
**Average price:** Modest
**Address:** Kingsway Court
Hove BN3 2LP
**Phone:** +44 1273 323810

#486

**Brighton Pagoda**
**Cuisines:** Chinese
**Average price:** Exclusive
**Address:** West Quay
Brighton Marina Village BN2 5UF
**Phone:** +44 1273 819053

#487
**Montefiore Fisheries**
**Cuisines:** Fish & Chips
**Average price:** Modest
**Address:** 23 Montefiore Road
Hove BN3 1RD
**Phone:** +44 1273 324496

#488
**Albert J Ramsbottom**
**Cuisines:** Fish & Chips
**Average price:** Inexpensive
**Address:** 58 Blatchington Road
Hove BN3 3YH
**Phone:** +44 1273 725551

#489
**Waggon & Horses**
**Cuisines:** Pub, British
**Average price:** Modest
**Address:** 109 Church St
Brighton BN1 1UD
**Phone:** +44 1273 602752

#490
**The Nevill of Hove**
**Cuisines:** Pub, Italian, Pizza
**Average price:** Modest
**Address:** 214 Nevill Road
Hove BN3 7QQ
**Phone:** +44 1273 558799

#491
**Cafe Coho**
**Cuisines:** Coffee, Tea, Breakfast & Brunch
**Average price:** Modest
**Address:** 83 Queen's Road
Brighton BN1 3XE
**Phone:** +44 1273 719126

#492
**Pizza Fritta**
**Cuisines:** Pizza, Italian
**Average price:** Inexpensive
**Address:** Churchill Square
Brighton and Hove BN1
**Phone:** +44 1273 719526

#493
**Hells Kitchen**
**Cuisines:** Deli, Coffee, Tea, Sandwiches
**Average price:** Modest
**Address:** 4 Gardner Street
Brighton BN1 1UP
**Phone:** +44 1273 604925

#494
**Truffles**
**Cuisines:** Bakery, Coffee, Tea,
Breakfast & Brunch
**Average price:** Modest
**Address:** 21 George Street
Hove BN3 3YA
**Phone:** +44 1273 725686

#495
**Pablo's**
**Cuisines:** Italian, Pizza
**Average price:** Inexpensive
**Address:** 36 Ship St
Brighton BN1 1AB
**Phone:** +44 1273 208123

#496
**Yummy Cottage**
**Cuisines:** Thai, Fast Food, Chinese
**Average price:** Modest
**Address:** 4 Leybourne Parade
Brighton and Hove BN2 4LW
**Phone:** +44 1273 818161

#497
**Gars Restaurant**
**Cuisines:** Chinese
**Average price:** Expensive
**Address:** 19 Prince Albert Street
Brighton BN1 1HF
**Phone:** +44 1273 321321

#498
**Caruso Restaurant**
**Cuisines:** Italian
**Average price:** Exclusive
**Address:** 70 Boundary Road
Hove BN3 5TD
**Phone:** +44 1273 277700

#499
**Hangleton Manor**
**Cuisines:** Pub, Gastropub, British
**Average price:** Expensive
**Address:** Hangleton Valley Drive
Hove BN3 8AN
**Phone:** +44 1273 413266

#500
**World Peace Cafe**
**Cuisines:** Coffee, Tea, Vegan
**Average price:** Modest
**Address:** 3 Landsdowne Road
Hove BN3 1DN
**Phone:** +44 1273 732917

Printed in Great Britain
by Amazon